A TIME FOR HONOR

A TIME FOR HONOR

A Portrait of
African American Clergywomen

DELORES C. CARPENTER

CHALICE
PRESS

St. Louis, Missouri

© Copyright 2001 by Delores C. Carpenter

Bible quotations, unless otherwise noted, are from the *New Revised Standard Version Bible,* copyright 1989, Division of Christian Education of the National Council of the Churches of Christ in the United States of America. Used by permission. All rights reserved.

Cover art: "A Touch of His Garment" by Thea Troupe
Cover design: Elaine Young
Interior design: Elizabeth Wright
Art direction: Michael Domínguez

This book is printed on acid-free, recycled paper.

Visit Chalice Press on the World Wide Web at
www.chalicepress.com

10 9 8 7 6 5 4 3 2 1   01 02 03 04 05 06

Library of Congress Cataloging-in-Publication Data

Carpenter, Delores Causion.
   A time for honor : a portrait of African American clergywomen /
Delores C. Carpenter.
      p. cm.
   Includes bibliographical references.
   ISBN 0-8272-3638-7 (alk. paper)
   1. African American women clergy.   I. Title.
   BR563.N4 C355 2001
   262'.14'08996073–dc21

                                                      2001000775

Printed in the United States of America

This book is dedicated to
my grandmother, Rev. Sarah Causion,
my mother, Mrs. Sarah Whye,
my two daughters, Jane and Susan,
and black clergywomen past and future.

Contents

List of Tables

Preface

African American clergywomen have been in the United States since the time of slavery. In the late twentieth century, an increasing number of black women began attending seminaries accredited by the Association of Theological Schools (ATS). This is the normative educational preparation required for ordination to Christian ministry within mainline Protestant churches of America and Canada.

Eventually the training of clergy was elevated to the graduate theological level and was offered only to those who had received a Bachelor's degree. Obtaining the professional ministerial degree—first the Bachelor of Divinity, which was later changed to the Master of Divinity—involves three years of full-time graduate academic work after college. Many students take more than three years, because they work and only go to school part-time. Thus, the ministry, which is the oldest of the professions, requires the same length of study as does the legal profession.

The matter of a "learned" clergy for the black church has long been called for by such denominations as the African Methodist Episcopal Church. Places such as Howard University School of Divinity, Virginia Union University Theological Seminary, and the Interdenominational Theological Center had long prepared black pastors and church leaders. But the larger numbers of black students entering theological education came when the Rockefeller Foundation and later the Fund for Theological Education (FTE) began to offer sizeable scholarships to black men and later to black women to help underwrite the high cost of attending such schools. In 1998, Howard University Divinity School cost $10,000 per year in tuition alone. A substantial amount of Lilly Endowment money helped FTE to offer Benjamin Mays Fellowships until the late 1990s, when funding was discontinued. With more financial help in place and with larger numbers of black students finishing college, the ranks of black ministers who could afford to do graduate theological study began to grow.

The other factor that attracted even higher numbers to the seminary was the offering of a full complement of evening and weekend classes so that seminarians could retain their current jobs and prepare for ministry without giving up their family's primary source of income. The evening and weekend classes coincided with the "graying of the clergy," that is, the fact that a larger and larger proportion of seminarians were second-career persons. They were older in age and were transferring into ministry after a career in another field for which they had previously trained. In this group now came more and more women. In some seminaries the female enrollment had reached fifty percent and beyond by 1995. The women were academically accomplished and raised the eyebrows of many within the academy and church. Faculty, administrators, students, and church officials alike confronted their own and others' perceptions and attitudes about women as ordained clergy.

This book is about three great powers: (1) the power of an educational credential to challenge ecclesiastical systems, (2) the power of critical numbers to change attitudes and social practices, and (3) the power of the "call" to ministry in the lives of black women. Today more and more black women are enrolling in seminary, graduating, being ordained, and setting their sights on full-time ministry. It is almost fashionable now for a large, urban black church whose pastor has a Masters or Doctoral degree to add an ordained, seminary-trained woman to the paid staff. This is one of the marks of an open-minded, progressive church that recognizes the gifts and talents of women.

In 1972, the Association of Theological Schools began to request a separate reporting of female enrollment within all member institutions. Thus, the possibility of a study such as this book describes was born. The continuing emergence of the leadership of black clergywomen can be tied to education. Education remains a strong key to the improvement of blacks in America. For many years, the black church did not require high levels of educational attainment for its pastors. But as more African American laity have gone to college and graduate school, they have expected that newly selected pastors have credentials on a par with those required in other professions, in government service, and in corporate America. As a black minister is interviewed to preside over a large congregation and budget, the committee is apt to ask the minister to present a five-year strategic plan to go with his or her vision for the church. This substantiates Charles Hamilton's thesis that in general, the black church expects its pastor to be a little better educated than its parishioners. It testifies also to the endurance of higher education as a core value within the black church. While some churches will always claim that education is not a determinant of ministry, there will also always be churches that highly regard it.

This book brings the black woman pastor to the foreground of consideration, and incorporates information about the black male minister as well. As more and more opportunities are opening to women, vital statistics in this book give the reader a portrait of contemporary African American clergywomen. It is time to honor these women. This volume illuminates their struggles and triumphs. This is a book about social change. It seeks to describe how the modern black church adapts to gender shifts in American culture and society.

Five case studies are included in the book. They are based on telephone interviews. The names have been changed to preserve the clergywomen's anonymity.

Acknowledgments

My research on the struggle of black clergywomen began more than twenty years ago, while I was a doctoral student at Rutgers University. It became the topic of my dissertation, of several publications, and of a lifelong passion. Accordingly, once a year I teach a course at Howard University School of Divinity entitled Women in Ministry. Both male and female seminarians from Howard as well as from Wesley Theological Seminary and Protestant Episcopal Theological Seminary in Virginia have expressed appreciation for a quantitative discussion of this important problem. I humbly thank the individuals and institutions that have encouraged me.

This endeavor began at a time when very little had been published on contemporary clergywomen. The three members of my doctoral dissertation committee were pivotal to my initial work. Dr. William Phillips chaired the committee. The Reverend Dr. Samuel Proctor, then pastor of Abyssinia Baptist Church in Harlem, New York, and the Reverend Dr. James Scott, recently retired pastor of Bethany Baptist Church in Newark, New Jersey, are the pastor/professors whom I have tried to emulate in my own academic and ministerial career.

I am also indebted to many colleagues who have been associated with Hartford Seminary, especially Dr. Adair Lummis. The watershed work *Women of the Cloth: A New Opportunity for the Churches,* by Jackson W. Carroll, Barbara Hargrove, and Adair T. Lummis, was invaluable to me. Over the years, several of the Hartford faculty have continued to collaborate in researching women in ministry. I have paid particular attention to their more recent publications, *Defecting in Place: Women Claiming Responsibility for their own Spiritual Lives,* by Miriam Therese Winter, Adair T. Lummis, and Allison Stokes, and *Clergywomen: An Uphill Calling,* by Barbara Brown Zikmund, Adair T. Lummis, and Patricia M. Y. Chang. These people have supported my work, and their support has kept me encouraged, visible, and vocal on this topic. My most recent interaction with the National Council of Churches' Women in Ministry Committee is in part due to their recommendation and the support of Rev. Denise Mason of the United Church of Christ. I am grateful for the small grant that the Women in Ministry Committee gave me, as well as an earlier small grant from the Lilly Endowment.

While still at Essex County College in Newark, I was propelled to finish this undertaking by some friends at the Cultural and Ecumenical Center of St. Johns University in Collegeville, Minnesota. Particular thanks go to Dr. J. Deotis Roberts and Bishop Thomas Hoyt, who first added me to the list of participants for three summers of confessional dialog. Out of this group, persons such as Dr. Cheryl Townsend Gilkes and Dr. Toinette Eugene have continued to publish articles and books on black women in the church and community.

I arrived at Howard University School of Divinity in 1982 while I was in the middle of my first data collection. Both Dean Lawrence Jones and my faculty colleagues stressed the importance of getting this information into print. After Dean Jones's retirement, Dean Clarence G. Newsome assisted me whenever possible. Along the way, it was my good fortune to receive a Faculty Excellence Grant from Howard University.

I thank Michigan Park Christian Church (Disciples of Christ) for granting me two sabbatical leaves to work on this book and on the *African Heritage Hymnal*, published in 2001 by GIA, Inc., in Chicago. These two three-month absences coincided with a year-long sabbatical from Howard University. Without some time away from teaching and pastoral responsibilities, I would have found it impossible to finish the basic research and writing. Over these many years, Howard University and Michigan Park Christian Church, which are situated across the street from one another, have become havens of love and helpfulness.

At the request of Chalice Press, I conducted a Summer 1999 study to update the data. This proved to be a labor of love that was dependent upon volunteers to help with the mailings. The long hours of intensive effort are most appreciated. My thanks are due to Dr. Julia Lacey, Rev. Alberta Johnson, Rev. Patricia Miller Johnson, Mrs. Sarah Whye, the Reverend Dr. Valerie Eley, Mrs. Velma Miller, Mrs. Barbara Lucas, and Mrs. Jane Thomas. Mrs. Patricia Wade did most of the typing. Jane Carpenter was indispensable in reading through most of the document, as was Minister Beverly Goines. Dr. Julia Lacey made many helpful comments. The primary statisticians for the research were John Jolly and Ivy Harrison. Their contributions were immeasurable, and mainly without compensation.

Finally, thanks to Dr. Jon L. Berquist, the Academic Editor of Chalice Press, who believed in the project and recognized the value of its publication. He has been very gracious. To God be the glory! Great things God has done!

1

Black Christian Women
in the African American Church

Black women have greatly influenced the direction, role, and leadership of the black church in social issues and action affecting the development and progress of African Americans in the United States since the days of enslavement. The increasing body of research to help persons and groups become familiar with the names and history of the contributions of noteworthy black women is affirming and encouraging. A few of such studies are noted here to indicate the scope of research undertaken. Dr. Jualynne Dodson focuses on black women in African Methodist Episcopal church history in her study that appears in *Women in New Worlds: Historical Perspectives on the Wesleyan Tradition*. The United Methodists produced one of the pioneering publications on black women, entitled *To a Higher Glory: The Growth and Development of Black Women Organized for Mission in the Methodist Church, 1940–1968*. This collaboration by Ruth C. Carter, Willa Curry, Mai H. Gray, Thelma McCallum, and Emma Wilson Strother documents the contributions of African American women in the Methodist Episcopal tradition from the time of slavery to the 1960s. Also, Dr. Cheryl Gilkes has recently published an important book, *If It Wasn't for the Women* (Orbis, 2001). Additionally, *Sisters of the Spirit* by William L. Andrews chronicles the ministries of Jarena Lee, Julia Foote, and Zepha Elaw. Other studies will be cited as this historical summary unfolds. Many scholars are now

1

describing the historical, sociological, biblical, theological, and homiletical contributions of black Christian women, both past and present (Carpenter 1986, Felder, Johnson, Mitchell 1988).

Late Nineteenth-Century Black Women in Ministry

It is impossible to study black women in ministry without mentioning some lesser-known predecessor laywomen, preachers, and pastors. It is highly probable that laywomen, such as the resolute Nannie Helen Burroughs, would have become ordained ministers had that opportunity been equitably available to them based on merit. The ordination of Pauli Murray, after many years as an active Episcopal laywoman, supports such judgment. This acknowledgment was granted toward the end of her life after her diligently seeking ordination over the years.

The United Methodists have traced the religious conversion activities of black females to slave women such as Mother Suma, who converted her mistress, one of the Boston Hancocks, and thereby raised the acceptance of Methodism in Boston (Carter et al.). Another slave woman of note was Aunt Hester of Franklin, Louisiana, whose constant preaching and praying was an annoyance to her master but had a salutary effect on other enslaved persons of the household. The master's discomfort prompted him to sell her twice, but the consternation that followed in the wake of her absence prompted him to repurchase her to restore calmness to his household. Upon her return, she continued to spread the word, causing even the young mistresses to become serious about religion and the master to acquiesce to her preaching and praying and spoiling of the negroes.

Other black abolitionists also spoke as ministers. The two religious giants, Harriet Tubman, the black female "Moses" of her people, and Sojourner Truth, the famous black Methodist preacher and abolitionist, have been much written about already. The accounts of their religious faith and church affiliation are well documented elsewhere (on Harriet Tubman, see Blassingame, Bradley, Conrad, and Powell; on Sojourner Truth, see Fauset, Gilbert, Ortiz, Pauli, Truth, and Vale). Another illustrious example is Maria Stewart, who was born in Hartford, Connecticut, in 1803. An orphan at five years old, she was assigned to work in a clergyman's family. She left this home at the age of fifteen. Although she had been previously denied an education, she spent the next five years in Sabbath Schools and wrote of her religious conversion in 1830. While preaching against slavery and teaching pride and self-help among blacks she called,

"O ye daughters of Africa, awake! Awake! Arise! No longer sleep or slumber, but distinguish yourselves, store thy mind with useful knowledge" (Stewart, 11). Eloquently and convincingly, she emphasized piety and knowledge.

> I have borrowed much of my language from the Holy Bible. During childhood and youth, it was the book that I mostly studied and now, while my hands are toiling for their daily sustenance, my heart is most generally meditating upon its divine truth. (Stewart, 24)

Because Maria Stewart spoke out on behalf of black women, she was hissed and reproached. She called on the women to make mighty efforts to raise their sons and daughters from servitude and degradation. She criticized the male clergy for crying, "Peace, peace when there was no peace, they have plastered us up with untempered mortar, and have been as it were blind leaders of the blind" (Stewart, 60).

Stewart repeatedly had to defend her right to preach in the churches.

> I believe, that for wise and holy purposes, best known to [God], [God] hath unloosed my tongue and put [divine] word into my mouth, in order to confound and put all those to shame that have rose up against me. For [God] hath clothed my face with steel, and lined my forehead with brass. [God] hath put [divine] testimony within me, and engraven [the divine] seal on my forehead. And with these weapons I have indeed set the fiends of earth and hell at defiance...Among the Greeks, women delivered the Oracles; the respect the Romans paid to the Sybils is well known. The Jews had their prophetesses. The predictions of the Egyptian women obtained much credit at Rome, even under the Emperors. And in the most barbarious [*sic*] nations, all things that have the appearance of being supernatural, mysteries of religion, the secrets of the psychic, and the rites of magic, were in the possession of women. Why cannot a religious spirit animate us now? (Stewart, 75)

Before Maria Stewart began her ministry in New England, another black woman preacher had emerged. Jarena Lee was born in 1784 at Cape May, New Jersey. She joined the African Methodist Episcopal (A.M.E) Church after hearing Reverend Richard Allen and experiencing conversion. When she felt called to preach, Reverend Allen told her of another Methodist woman, a Mrs. Cook, who had done well in exhortation and holding prayer meetings by verbal license of the preacher in charge. However, he said, there was no provision for women to preach. Nonetheless, eight years later, Bishop Allen affirmed Jarena Lee's calling, and she became the first female preacher in the A.M.E Church. She worked in Bethel Church in Philadelphia and traveled extensively. In four years she traveled 1,600 miles, of which she walked 1,100 miles, to carry out her ministry. Bishop Allen wanted to give her an appointment at Bethel Church, but the opposition against a woman preaching blocked her appointment. Still, she preached in schoolhouses, at slave camp meetings, and in homes as well as churches in Pennsylvania, New York, New Jersey, Virginia, and Maryland. She was sometimes asked to fill in when the preacher did not show up, but she also faced enormous aversion from elders and local magistrates in her travels. Mrs. Lee wrote, "At times I was pressed down like a cart beneath its shafts—my life seemed as at the point of the sword—my heart was sore and pained me in my body" (Lee).

Early in church history, black women took a particular interest in missionary work in Africa. Thus, they assumed leadership positions long ago. Francis Burns in 1834, Lavinia Johnson in 1845, and Sarah Simpson in 1860 were missionaries to Liberia. In 1902 Susan Collins and in 1906 Martha Drummer went to Angola as Methodist missionaries. All these women worked in the mission field until they retired (Carter et al., 36–40).

The pastor's wife has been another highly visible source of leadership within the black church. One early example was Charlotte Forten Grimke, wife of Francis Grimke, the pastor of Fifteenth Street Presbyterian Church in Washington, D.C. The daughter of a prominent black Philadelphia family, Charlotte Forten was educated at the Salem Normal School in Massachusetts and taught for the Freedmen's Bureau in South Carolina. While on this assignment, she spent time on an island in the neighborhood of Beaufort. She described in the *Atlantic Monthly* in 1864 the culture of those she went to serve. Religion was central to their lives, and her writings preserve some of the lyrics of their hymns:

> The people of this island have no songs. They sing only hymns and most of them are sad. Prince, a large Black boy from a neighboring plantation was the principal shouter

among the children. Amaretta's favorite hymn is one of the oldest we have heard: "What makes ol Satan follow me so? Satan got nuttin tall fur to do wid me; Tidy Rosa, hold your light; Brudder Tony, hold your light; All de member, hold your light on Canaan's shore!" (Grimke, 97)

Charlotte Forten later moved to Washington, D.C., where she joined Fifteenth Street Presbyterian Church in 1877 and married in 1879. By then she had become a renowned poet and writer, as well as an art and literature critic. Frequently she wrote in defense of black people.

Many black women began their ministries as evangelists. Such a woman was Amanda Smith. Born in slavery, Amanda Smith was working as a washerwoman in 1870 when she felt led by God to go to an evangelistic meeting. Converted as a young woman, she found "sanctification"—the perfection of holiness—in September of 1868 under John Inskip's preaching at his Greene Street Church in New York. She began to attend camp meetings around the East, testifying and singing, mostly with white Pentecostals. She said God saved many from prejudice under her ministry. Once, she attended a national camp meeting in Knoxville, Tennessee, where the session had been in progress for three days without success. However, after she gave her testimony, one of the leading opponents of holiness began to weep. Stepping onto the platform, he told how many years he had been a Methodist minister and how prejudiced against the subject of holiness he had been.

> When I heard this colored sister tell how God had led her and brought her into this blessed experience, the darkness swept away and God has saved me, and I see truth as I never did before. Glory to God! (Ruether and McLaughlin, 237; cf. Smith)

Amanda Smith took her message of holiness to the British Isles as well. She also traveled to India where the Methodist bishop observed,

> She possessed a clearness of vision which I have found seldom equalled…During seventeen years that I have lived in Calcutta, I have found many famous strangers to visit the city, but I have never known anyone who could draw and hold so large an audience as Mrs. Smith. (Ruether and McLaughlin, 237)

She also spent a number of years in Africa, particularly in Liberia. When she finally felt too old to travel, Amanda Smith returned to the United States in 1890 and founded an orphanage near Chicago, where she served until her death in 1915.

Twentieth-Century Black Women in Ministry

Other African American women started churches of their own in the last century. Lucy Smith was born in 1875 in Georgia. She migrated to Atlanta in 1909 and relocated a few years later to Chicago. Reared a Baptist, she made her way to Stone Church, a white Pentecostal fellowship. In 1914 she received her calling to divine healing. She began her meetings in her home and in the 1930s established the All Nations Pentecostal Church. Elder Smith said,

> Come to my Church more often and witness how many hundreds of men and women I heal—all kinds of sores and pains of the body and of the mind. I heal with prayers—jus' lay my hand on troubled place and pray, and it all goes away…I started giving advice to folks in my neighborhood. This made me realize how much a good talking does to many people. Very soon they started coming more and more and so for the last seven years, I've been preaching to large numbers…The members of my church are troubled and need something to make them happy. My preaching is not about sad things but always about being saved. The singing in my church has "swing" to it, because I want my people to swing out of themselves all the misery and troubles that is heavy on their hearts. (Washington, 66–67)

In the 1890s some black women volunteered to teach in the Freedmen Aid Society through their denominations. Some went to work in the South. Realizing that they could not serve on the Freedmen's Board of Directors, the Methodist women turned their minds to playing a larger role. The activities of their Women's Home Missionary Society supplemented the Freedmen Aid Society and won acclaim for its accomplishments, including providing for the education of black girls, for childcare, and for general evangelism.

Many black congregations supported these types of activities, though women's rights in church were hotly debated in both the late nineteenth and early twentieth centuries. For example, the highest legislating bodies of the three denominations that eventually made up The United Methodist Church did not officially seat women until 1892, 1900, and 1902. Full clergy rights for women in this church were not achieved until 1956.

Beginning in 1888, a small number of black women were commissioned as deaconesses. Their ministries stressed work with destitute persons and groups in urban areas. An outstanding example of such a worker, Anna Hall was the first black graduate deaconess of the African Methodist Episcopal Church. Commissioned in 1901, she started a city mission in Atlanta and supervised the fieldwork of Clark College female students. After five years, Anna Hall went to Liberia, where she stayed for twenty-four years. She was "everything to the people–farmer, teacher, preacher, doctor, dentist, nurse and evangelist" (Carter et al., 37). The Liberian Church named a mission station for her in 1952. In 1954 the Anna E. Hall Apartments for married students were dedicated at Gammon Theological Seminary in Atlanta.

In 1909 Viola Mae Young wrote, "And from a child I have loved the church and have felt I was a preacher's friend!" (Young, 1). Miss Young echoes the great host of black women who have endeavored to work in the area of pastor's aid and pastoral relations. She joined the AME Church in 1899 at the age of twelve and worked to help laymen better understand the minister's message. She established the practice of repeating the minister's text to members after each service until many others in the congregation began to pay closer attention to it and frequently recall it. She also began to keep a calendar of all the minister's appointments so that the members would not forget them. Her book *Little Helps for Pastors and Members,* a practical guide to pastors and members, was published in Rosebud, Alabama, in 1909.

Baptist women were recognized in the early 1900s as elocutionists, lecturers, field secretaries for the Women's Conventions, missionary workers, teachers, writers, training school directors, Bible Band workers, and orators. Included in *Who's Who Among the Colored Baptists in the United States* in 1913 was Ida Becks of Missouri, a fearless advocate of women's suffrage and defender of African Americans (Bacote). She became secretary of the Colored Women's League of Dayton, Ohio. Also listed is Mrs. M. A. B. Smith of Texas, who was director of the Guadalupe Training School. Women of the Baptist churches supported the teacher for this school. Ella Whitfield, Matron at Guadalupe College, became a field worker in Miss Joanna Moore's Bible Band. Remarkably, she delivered 491 addresses, visited 823 homes and 312 churches, and collected $2,009 for the church (Bacote,

101–3, 249–50, 258–60). L. J. McNorton, who took millinery and dressmaking classes in Chicago and St. Louis, taught these skills to other black women. She eventually operated a successful business in Ft. Worth, Texas.

Minnie Moxley became a high school teacher in Waco, Texas, and was famous for her ability to inspire her students. Annie Wilkins became head teacher at Hearne Academy, Houston College, after serving as industrial teacher at Bishop College. Mrs. T. Castle, founder of Rescue Home in Byram, Texas, was an apostle of temperance. She enrolled over 160 clients and raised, with the help of the church, $6,000 to purchase eleven acres of land with a nine-room residence for her young people. Josie B. Hall taught public schools when she was only sixteen, and she also distinguished herself as a poet and writer. All the women mentioned here gave great energy and time to the Baptist church. Although the information about them is sketchy, it remains a tribute to their varied contributions that they are remembered as prominent churchwomen.

One famous Baptist woman about whom much more is recorded is Nannie Helen Burroughs. Born in 1879 in Washington, D.C., Nannie Burroughs founded the first Girl's Literary Society of the public high schools and wrote for leading newspapers and journals of the day. Converted at the age of fifteen, she joined Nineteenth Street Baptist Church and held many offices in the congregation. Working as a stenographer, she was elected president of the National Training School for Women. She traveled throughout America giving brilliant speeches, which emphasized that listeners must "do ordinary things in an extraordinary manner" (Bacote, 240). By way of example, in three years she raised the assets of her school from $6,000 to $35,000. She took a vital interest in Africa and was the leader of the Young Women's Department of the National Association of Colored Women's Clubs. Under her leadership much was done to get blacks to vote. Burroughs urged black women to take their families to the polls to vote for those issues and persons who were working on behalf of the uplift of the race. Thus, she became a political as well as religious leader (Brooks).

In the religious arena, probably the most enduring contribution of Nannie Helen Burroughs was encouraging churches to establish Woman's Day observances. Writing in a monograph, she described how this great tradition started within the black church. She first presented the idea, purpose, and plan of Woman's Day in Memphis, Tennessee, in September 1906 as part of her report as corresponding secretary of the Woman's Convention Auxiliary to the National Baptist Convention. Since the work of the convention had hardly begun, Nannie Burroughs was dubbed an "upstart," to which unkind thrust she was provoked to answer, "I might be an 'upstart,' but I am also starting up." The convention eventually voted to accept the "Woman's Day" resolution. The purpose of this national observance day was to interest women of the local churches in raising money for foreign missions, the chief interest of the Woman's Convention at that time. It was intended to be not a scheme for raising money but an effort primarily designed for "raising" women. Nannie Helen Burroughs suggested that, in order to interest and develop the women, the secretary be permitted to prepare and send out the Woman's Day program and three special addresses (short but challenging) on missions or on some kindred phase of that subject and that the speeches be based on firsthand, current information about the missionary enterprise. It was pointed out that the material for the addresses furnished would be committed to memory by speakers selected by the Missionary Society and, thus, the convention could discover and develop public speakers for church programs, particularly for Woman's Day.

Woman's Day eventually proved to be equally as successful in raising money as in expanding the ranks of black women church leaders. Dr. Adam C. Powell, Sr., pastor of Abyssinian Baptist Church, New York City, had the following to say to a great Sunday morning audience: "As much as the churches have gained from Nannie Burroughs's idea of WOMAN'S DAY and from her famous play 'THE SLABTOWN CONVENTION,' every church ought to set aside one Sunday in the year to be known as 'NANNIE BURROUGHS' DAY,' and send this woman every dollar they raise on that one day in the year to endow and operate the school which she founded for women and girls at Washington, D.C."

Continuing, Dr. Powell said:

> The churches owe it to her because we are all getting more money off of her idea of WOMAN'S DAY and her play "THE SLABTOWN CONVENTION," than we are getting from any other idea given to the churches in this generation. (Burroughs)

The Nannie Helen Burroughs School stands today as a community center in far northeast Washington, D.C., as a monument to this great churchwoman. Another tribute, the Nannie Helen

Burroughs Scholarship Fund, established at Howard University School of Divinity, has assisted many female seminarians. For many years it was the only scholarship available to women at this institution.

Over time, Woman's Day came to be referred to as Women's Day. The institution of Women's Day is very significant for African American female ministers, because when pulpits first opened to women preachers, it was usually within the context of Women's Day. Well over half their preaching was done in the course of traveling to different churches to speak for Women's Day. This, coupled with the evangelistic preaching of revivals, was the only opportunity for most women to preach until recently. At present, there are still many black congregations that hear a woman speak only on Women's Day. Initially, professional laywomen were preferred speakers on this day. Within the past four decades (1960s, 1970s, 1980s, and 1990s), it became more and more common to invite an ordained or licensed woman minister, frequently referred to as "a lady preacher."

Christian Education and Professional Church Leadership

In April 1913, Matilda Moseley, then superintendent of twenty-three colored schools in Cumberland County, Virginia, trudged in and out of Sunday schools and churches seeking assistance in building eight new schools and remodeling thirteen others. Looking back on her success in this building drive she said, "Every school I have been able to remodel or build had its beginning in some church or Sunday School where I have taken pride to work irrespective of denomination" (Jeness, 30). Later, she and her husband led the effort to rebuild their church meetinghouse. Matilda Moseley Booker eventually moved to Mecklenburg County, where she was instrumental in securing grants from the Rosenwald Fund to match local funds to build sixteen new schools for blacks.

The longest tenured black staff member of the Methodist Episcopal Church, Hattie R. Hargis of Wilmington, Delaware, was elected as head of the Bureau of Friendship Homes in 1928. Friendship Home in Cincinnati was a national facility for black girls away from home. Another in Philadelphia provided safe housing, childcare, and nutritional guidance for its residents.

Bethlehem Centers, many of which continue today as community centers in ethnic minority and disadvantaged neighborhoods, were an early twentieth-century product of Southern black churchwomen. The Sarah D. Murphy Home in Cedartown, Georgia, today a facility for emotionally disturbed black children and youth, resulted from the labors of Sarah D. Murphy, who began taking children into her home in 1932.

Bethune Cookman College in Daytona Beach, Florida, was a Methodist Episcopal school rooted in the Freedmen Aid Society and Woman's Society of Christian Service. Its founder, Dr. Mary McLeod Bethune, proudly identified herself as a Methodist woman in mission. Speaking in 1933 she said:

> It may be safely said that the chief sustaining force in support of the pulpit and the various phases of missionary enterprise has been the feminine element of the membership. The development of the Negro church since the Civil War has been another of the modern miracles. Throughout its growth the untiring effort, the unflagging enthusiasm, the sacrificial contribution of time, effort, and cash earnings of the black woman have been the most significant factors, without which the modern Negro church would have no history worth the writing. (Lerner, 573; cf. Newsome 1981, 1982)

The Christian Methodist Episcopal (CME) women take great pride in names like Helena Cobb and Dr. Mattie Coleman. In 1934 their women's magazine, *The Messenger,* had a circulation of 3,000. Mrs. R. T. Hollis, the Connectional President for CME women said:

> The church woman, as such, should have the conviction that they, as individuals and as a group, should take the lead and point the way to progress, social progress, economic progress, spiritual progress. We should be the first to cooperate with trends to bring about justice to all people and fair play in a war torn world…We as women, are not clamoring merely for recognition in church and world movements, we want to fulfill our destiny. We are destined to play a major role in the destiny of humanity, for women represent the cooperative spirit in life. (McAfee, 464)

Most Sunday school teachers in the black church have been women. Black women who taught in the public schools almost always shared their talents as Sunday school teachers, but they also distinguished themselves as Christian educators in a larger sense. In 1936 Mary Jeness published a book, *Twelve Negro Americans,* in which she spotlighted outstanding black adults unfamiliar to most black students, and young blacks whose youthful accomplishments pointed toward greatness. The Council of Women for Home Missions and

Missionary Education Movement commissioned Ms. Jeness to write a study companion as a supplemental guide to her book. It was entitled *A Course for Intermediates on the Negro in America.*

Another young black woman who started her career as a Christian educator was Dorothy I. Height. In 1948 she and J. Oscar Lee wrote for the Young Women's Christian Association (YWCA) and Federal Churches of Christ *The Christian Citizen and Civil Rights: A Guide to Study and Action.* The guide was based on the report of the President's Committee on Civil Rights, *To Secure These Rights.* Leaders of churches and Christian associations nationwide used this book in their efforts to secure civil rights. In the 1960s, Dorothy Height planned and conducted workshops for the YWCA all over the United States based on the organization's imperative, "to eliminate racism by whatever means necessary." At the same time she became president of the National Council of Negro Women.

By the end of World War II, black churchwomen saw new visions and opportunities, generally, and thus began to call for more black professional churchwomen in leadership positions. At a meeting at Gulfside, Mississippi, an executive of the Methodist women in 1945, a Mrs. Bowen, captured the mood:

> Let us face the true facts. We are all hard working people and do not have the time nor the funds to do what is actually needed to be done. There is a need for a worker in each district to sell ideas and the program of the Woman's Society of Christian Service to pastors and women of our rural churches, and to assist in organizing them, and then to make an occasional follow up of the work. (Carter et al., 44)

Following in this same tradition, Pauli Murray was commissioned by the United Methodists' Christian Social Relations and Local Church Activities to study the scope of discrimination in the United States. Her 1951 publication, *States' Laws on Race and Color,* awakened many Christian women to the need to change unjust state laws. Miss Murray later completed her doctorate in law and taught in the Yale University Law School and at the University of Ghana at Accra. She eventually became the first black woman to be ordained by the Episcopal Church. Her autobiography, *Song in a Weary Throat,* depicts the crusading and humanist spirit of Rev. Pauli Murray, a giant in the struggle for civil rights and the rights of women in the church (Murray 1987).

Another influential book written by an inspired Christian that appeared in 1951 was *Color Ebony* by Helen Caldwell Day. The beautiful story of this black Catholic laywoman's life inspired many, arguing that the whole problem of racism results from a misunderstanding and misapplication of Christian principles.

One noteworthy account in her book describes her effort to found a house of hospitality patterned after that of Dorothy Day's Catholic Worker in Memphis, Tennessee. Her association with a study group formed of black and white, Catholics and non-Catholics, with the purpose of considering social problems in the light of the church's teaching, clarified her plan. With the cooperation of the group, Blessed Martin House took shape. It was a house of hospitality, especially for the children of poor, working women, black and white. Blessed Martin House was "a place where laymen or laywomen or both have gone to give themselves to God through voluntary poverty and to practice the works of mercy; to serve the needs of the poor and their own spiritual needs" (Day, 3).

Dr. Olivia B. Stokes became the first black woman to earn a doctorate in Christian education from Columbia University in 1952. She was also the first black woman minister ordained in the National Baptist denomination. During her exemplary career, she taught at Andover Newton Seminary, Colgate Rochester Seminary, Harvard Divinity School, and New York University.

Dr. Stokes's example of leadership may be favorably compared with that of Anna Arnold Hedgeman, who began her career as a YWCA worker, first in Ohio, then as a branch executive in the Jersey City YWCA, and as membership secretary at the Harlem Branch YWCA of the City of New York, and who then became a national figure in civil rights and politics. She held a responsible position in the planning of the 1963 March on Washington. She wrote to A. Philip Randolph, the director of the march,

> In light of the role of Negro women in the struggle for freedom and especially in light of the extra burden they have carried, because of the castration of our Negro man in this culture, it is incredible that no woman should appear as a speaker at the historic March on Washington meeting at the Lincoln Memorial. (Hedgeman, 179)

As a result of such lobbying, black women sat on the dais and made remarks.

The accomplishments of black Christian women have become even more spectacular in recent years. Theresa Hoover, formerly a Methodist Episcopal women's field-worker, in 1968 became associate general secretary of the Women's Division of the United Methodist Church's Board of Global Ministries. Few black women before her equaled her influence in the Christian world. Rev. Yvonne Delk, also a Christian educator, served as the first black woman to head the Church and Society Division of the United Church of Christ. She went on from there to serve as Executive of the Chicago Mission Society until her retirement. The United Methodists elected their first black woman bishop, Rev. Leontyne Kelley. In 2000, three African American clergywomen were elevated to bishop in the United Methodist Church. They are Violet Fisher, Linda Lee, and Beverly Shamana. Also, in 1988 in Boston, Massachusetts, the Episcopal Church consecrated its first female bishop—a black woman, Rev. Barbara Harris. Finally, in 2000, the Reverend Dr. Vashti McKenzie was elected the first black female bishop in the African American Church.

A Profile: A Contradiction and a Transition

Josephine Carson describes the Southern woman in the black church in *Silent Voices: The Southern Negro Woman Today,* published in 1969. Ms. Carson interviewed men and women throughout the South in the latter part of the 1960s. Some of the comments made about the role of men and women in the black church led her to an interesting conclusion.

Describing a church service in Atlanta, she writes:

> There are elders and deacons and one deaconess on the platform below the choir—an intensely black deaconess with straight waxy hair just below the ears, glasses, good posture, womanliness, and propriety. Her hands fold in her lap. Her feet stationed as guardsmen in double file. This one lone deaconess among the Protestant patriarchs has great dignity...He names now finally the Name of Names: "Gee-zuss! Gee-zuss!" And the deaconess cries out from a head that casts wildly about, a deranged mare, gasping for breath with which to call: Yes! Jesus! Amen! (Carson, 108)

Ms. Carson observes that the men show more restraint. "Praise in song is apparently easier for a man—that and long eloquent preaching. Perhaps the women shout and 'thrash and fallout' in the service more often than men because they do not have the privilege nor the restriction offered by preaching" (Carson, 122).

A woman in South Carolina speaks:

Here the church is all a man's domain and the women really don't have much to say. They do a lot of work, they cook for picnics and socials, and they raise the most money and they kind of keep the church going, but when you get to policy, the men have it all tied up. They don't want a woman in any kind of power. (Carson, 189)

The idea that black men feel entitled to leadership in the black church grows out of many years of patriarchal tradition wherein black men and women became accustomed to this entitlement for men. As black women begin to compete for some of these policy-making positions, it is understandable that men will view this movement as an erosion of their power and control. Coupled with the fact that there are few other opportunities for black men to inherit leadership outside the black church, resistance against women moving into the hierarchy emerges as a strongly embedded, intransigent barrier.

Often black women reinforce this barrier in their desire to have strong, black male role models in their lives. The relationship between these women and their pastors can be very significant, with varying levels of intimacy, as they depend on these men for guidance, comfort, healing, nurture, closeness, and support. Add to this their respect for the sacred dimension of the "man of God," and women find a certain security in knowing that their spiritual well-being is entrusted to one who incarnates the presence of God. The image of God as Father imparts a very strong association in some women's minds with the images of their own fathers. This image is readily transferred to the male minister. Additionally and regrettably, most black women, observing the relative powerlessness of all black women in our world where men demand far greater respect, transfer this consciousness into an exalted image of the male preacher. This exalted image restores black women's confidence in black men in general, and, in turn, offers hopefulness in the face of societal and media emasculation of the black male. Given the inordinate focus on black men who are unemployed, physically abusive, incarcerated, drug dealers, drug addicts, or gay, there is a need to identify strong male figures who speak with authority, wield power, and display moderate affluence. If a woman is a single parent, it is increasingly important that her child or children have exposure to such a figure. Beneath a sacred canopy, the male pastor shepherds his flock with both compassion and authority. The highest source of power–spiritual power–illuminates his public words and deeds. He becomes a magnet, drawing large numbers of black women.

Other factors militating against the acceptance of women pastors will be explored in the next section of this article. Biblical texts are interpreted to prescribe women to certain roles, prohibiting the pastorate. Women are described as unable to fulfill the strenuous demands of the pastorate during pregnancy and menstruation. The arduous, sometimes confrontational nature of pastoral duties is viewed as leading women to lose their femininity and to diminish their womanhood. Such biblical, biological, and cultural definitions of women shape the current debate. Philosophical and theological considerations include the woman's place in the order of creation and dominant metaphors of the church, such as that of the bride. How does gender relate to this feminine metaphor of the church? The next several decades will reexamine these issues and others. The church stands to gain much needed biblical, theological, and cultural reflection as a result.

Asked why she considered black women to be segregated by the church, a woman in South Carolina responds,

> Well for one thing that's the only place a colored man can be strong. He doesn't have any power, any place else. This movement is changing things but it will be many a year before you see a colored man with influence, generally speaking, in this world. So he'll swing it all into the church where he can order all the people around and put down the law the way he wants. (Carson, 265)

Comments such as these led Carson to conclude that the "black woman is a worker, a woman who, although poor, can imagine and approve of women in almost any work or role except that of preacher" (Carson, 271).

As Carson's book was being published, the National Council of Churches gained support from a number of denominations to sponsor the first National Consultation of Ethnic Women in Ministry. These black, Hispanic, Asian, and American Indian churchwomen came from fifteen denominations. They worked in twenty-three different church-related occupations. They were seminarians, pastors, campus ministers, communication specialists, directors of national and regional church departments, seminary professors, administrators, and theologians, as well as local church program coordinators.

Forty-four black women from across the country were in the group. They met as a separate black caucus at the consultation and reported on the following needs:

1. to combine feminism with religious activities
2. to encourage black churches to minister to the whole community as well as particular congregations
3. to establish an intimate partnership between female clergy and laity
4. to eliminate ageism in every enterprise
5. to save black children through unity and community
6. to require a mandatory, creative, experimental course in Christian education in all seminaries
7. to meet separately as black women in ministry periodically while uniting permanently with all ethnic women in ministry (Carpenter 1968)

This was a historic meeting, in that it marked the first time that such a broadly representative group of black clergywomen gathered together to envision the future of the black church and to set their own agenda. It was to take its place in ushering in the progress that black clergywomen made in the seventies and the eighties. The staff person, Carolyn Showell, had brought together seminary and non-seminary trained ministers and rehearsed their "herstory." Pentecostal women participated. Pauli Murray even appeared on the program. Here, African American clergywomen were empowered to think beyond their own denominations, and expressed great interest in developing a national interest organization. Although the organization did not materialize, a new kind of networking had begun. The 1970s thus brought about a new era in the history of black churchwomen. By the eighties, the proactive results of the dialogue and conceptualizations of the previous two decades would be evident.

Progress toward New Differentiation: The Black Woman as Pastor, Associate Pastor, and Seminary Professor

The pioneering work of black women ministers in the 1980s and 1990s continues to aim for the open access of women to associate, sole, and senior pastor positions in the new century. Many black women seminarians are preparing for these career goals. The author's dissertation on this subject revealed that among black female seminary graduates nationally, 45 percent targeted a career in the parish ministry at the time they completed the Master of Divinity degree. When this figure is compared to the 12 percent who were pastoring in 1985 and the 20 percent who were associate pastors, it is clear that substantial change in the ministry ranks must continue (Carpenter 1986, 68, 70). As with other professions, the growing number of women finishing seminary and being accepted into the profession is a potent factor in such change, as well as with change in the roles of women in the larger society (Kanter; cf. Kanter and Millman, 49).

One of the most enlightening books on this subject is *The Black Church in the African American Experience.* Dr. C. Eric Lincoln and Dr. Lawrence H. Mamiya conducted two thousand interviews in urban areas with clergy from the seven historically black denominations–African Methodist Episcopal, African Methodist Episcopal Zion, Christian Methodist Episcopal, National Baptist USA Inc., National Baptist of America Unincorporated, Progressive Baptist, and Church of God in Christ. During this study 1,009 urban clergy were asked, "Would you approve of a woman as the pastor of a church?" Forty-nine percent approved and 51 percent disapproved. Only 14 percent strongly approved, while 28 percent strongly disapproved. Thirty-five percent merely approved and 24 percent merely disapproved. In sum, not only did the majority disapprove, but also the intensity of the disapproval was greater than the intensity of the approval. Of the 14 percent who strongly approved, 2 percent were the female clergy in the sample (Lincoln and Mamiya).

It is instructive to look at reasons that the clergy in the Lincoln-Mamiya study gave for disapproval and approval of black women pastors. Those who disapproved generally cited a biblical example, such as: There were no women among the twelve disciples (Mt. 10:2–4); Eve, a woman, was responsible for the downfall of man (Gen. 3:12), besides which she was created after man to be a helpmate (Gen. 2:18); Pauline epistles make references to women keeping silent in the church (1 Cor. 14:34) and to man being the head of the woman (1 Cor. 11:3) and wives being subject to their husbands (Eph. 5:22). Others cited their denomination's restrictions and, still others, the physical limitations of women. The following are sample responses:

She can be a "pastor's helper"–but God didn't make her job to be a pastor; they may have the educational ability, but they're not God-approved.

Theoretically [they have] co-equal positions but no women are pastors. "Spiritual leaders" or "church mothers" are female counterparts to ministers; other positions [are] held–deaconesses, missionaries.

[The] responsibility of pastor is too strenuous for women. The pastor is on call twenty-four hours, but there are certainly times when women are incapacitated, i.e., during pregnancy, during times of menstrual cycle.

However, I feel a woman can be an "evangelist." Deacons must do "dirty work"–how can you expect a woman to do such? She loses her femininity and it diminishes her womanhood.

In order to be a pastor, one must be blameless and the husband of one wife (that's what the Bible says), and there is no way a woman can be the husband of one wife. I don't care what kind of operation she has. [The biblical references, 1 Tim. 3:2 and Titus 1:6, actually state "bishop."]

When a woman brings a message, she is preaching. But when it comes to pastoring, it's not her place, according to the Bible.

In her discourse [she] can go whatever route she chooses to go to make plain the Gospel, but [I do] not call it preaching, I call it teaching. (Lincoln and Mamiya)

In the Lincoln-Mamiya study, the clergy who approved of women as pastors either cited other biblical examples, such as Galatians 3:28 ("There is no longer male and female"), or relied on the theological argument that God is all-powerful and can do anything. Many of those who approved also had direct experiences with women preachers and pastors. One pastor even made the analogy between racial discrimination and sexual discrimination.

In terms of biblical examples, Mary and Martha are called the first bearers of the good news of the resurrection (Mt. 28:1–8; Mk. 16:9–11; Lk. 24:1–10; Jn. 20:1–18). The following are remarks cited in the study in support of women pastors.

[God] called [Baalam's mule] to prophesy (Num. 22:28–31).

If the Lord can cause the rocks to cry out, surely he can call women (Lk. 19:40).

Adam and Eve—If woman (Eve) can lead men to hell, why can't she lead them to heaven? (Gen. 3:12). Value is not determined by sex.

I don't think God is a sexist. Men must not do to women what whites have done to us on the basis of a false anthropological view of human nature in a backward sociology.

I cannot restrict God to [the] male population of the Church. The Holy Spirit on the day of Pentecost was not discriminatory. There are varied ministries and room in those also.

I am a woman. I understand women to be more thorough and genuine in caring and nurturing.

They are my fellow yokemen. I strongly approve. I would be happy to serve under a woman pastor.

I think women have a place in the Christian ministry, although presently I am still mentally studying this situation in my own mind. I am convinced, however, God cannot be limited as to who he might call into his service.

The Bible, when interpreted through the eyes of Christ, is clearly opposed to all forms of sexism—as much as it is opposed to all forms of racism. In Christ there are no differences. Women remain women but are free to be persons—as I see it. (Lincoln and Mamiya)

Dr. Mamiya summarized the findings in a preliminary report to the Howard University School of Divinity. The data indicate that the majority of the membership of the mainline black denominations consists of women, with a ratio of 2.5–3 females to every male, yet the pastors are predominately male. An informed guess is that fewer than 5 percent of the clergy in the seven historically black denominations are female. In some major cities there are one or two women who lead large congregations of two to three thousand members, but, in every case, these are independent churches. There are probably five thousand black women ministers in independent storefront or house churches across America. Some of these women are bishops and head more than one congregation.

The finding that 8 percent of the urban clergy interviewed in the Lincoln-Mamiya study favor allowing women to pastor must be viewed with caution (Lincoln and Mamiya). This statistic is probably denominationally biased. While the Methodists and Progressive National Baptists allow women to practice ministry to the same extent as men, the Church of God in Christ and other Baptists restrict women to prescribed areas outside the ordained ministry. The struggle for black women to become pastors and paid associate pastors in some other mainline black denominations is fraught with difficulty.

Contemporary Images of a Black Woman Minister

When Howard University School of Divinity held its first Women in Ministry Conference in 1983, a black radio talk show in Washington, D.C., opened its lines to the public on the issue of women ministers (Tate). The first three calls were negative reactions; all others were in support of women preachers and pastors. The following three statements are either representative or reported verbatim:

A man said,

> I disagree [with] women in ministry. A man should be the head...Jesus is coming back for a bride. The Church is the bride, so there is no place for women ministers. But if man does not do what he should, dominate the earth, I don't know about these women. I just don't believe in them. (Tate)

A woman said,

> I am definitely against female ministers in the pulpit. The Bible is our road map. There is not one example, saying female preaching...Women ministers use all kinds of examples to justify that they were called to the ministry. They say the women were always present. Women can help, as Eve was a helpmeet. It's very clear in Scripture that man was not made for woman, but woman for man. Just as Jesus is head of the Church, man is head of a woman. No female should be in the pulpit. We can be ministers of a kind, as missionaries. Utilizing these gifts does not mean preaching

from the pulpit like a man, being in the pulpit. That force that will not allow women in the pulpit—I hope they will stand on the Word and not allow women to be ordained or in the pulpit. (Tate) [Most likely she is referring to the largest local ministers' conference, which has consistently disapproved of women ministers and dismissed male ministers who ordain women or are ordained at the same time as women.]

A man said,

I believe in women preachers because my pastor is a woman. And she is the most "beautifulest" person I ever came into contact with in all my life. If God can speak to an ass, he can use a woman...I believe that the women—God has chosen them because these men out here are so hard-hearted and they don't want to do the work. (Tate)

Rev. Blanche Allen ended the radio show by saying:

The specification of ministry is that it is for God...God is an appointing God and God appoints whomever [God] will. Jonah was a reluctant prophet. But God appointed the gourd and the whale and the worm. These are very serious times. We do not have the luxury of being dissenting persons. We need to be busy helping people. There are many who have a mandate to heal and counsel. Jesus reminded the people that they had killed the prophets. He said that God would have gathered them like a Mother Hen, had they been open to it. (Tate)

As the black female leadership, both clergy and lay, becomes better educated and more conscious of discrimination within the black church, confrontations will occur in denominations that do not listen to the voices of black women within religious institutions. Exposed to new gains by their white sisters, some black church-women are facing tremendous conflict. In some cases, ordination is still prohibited. Frequently, church-related employment remains token or nonexistent for women. But black women are determined to find new places within religious institutions. Some will leave the faith communities in which they first discovered and developed their talents and spiritual gifts. They will seek newer and more fruitful opportunities elsewhere.

Key to the resolution of the problem of black women in the pastorate is the growing cadre of black women who now hold full-time faculty positions in theological schools. They are bringing fresh scholarship and "womanist" perspectives to the academic disciplines that they teach.[1] Many of them are writing about this issue in the popular domain. In their writing and in their teaching, they are influencing the thinking of male and female ministers who come under their tutelage, and they are bringing greatly needed insight to biblical and theological interpretations that attempt to discern what God is calling the church to be in the twenty-first century. Many of these women professors are ordained. Some of them have been or are presently serving as pastors. Their responses to the question, What is the appropriate role of black women in the church today? will greatly influence the thinking of future ministers. Further, the fact that men and women are preparing for ministry together is very significant. It seems that social change and a new theological awareness are inevitable.

The black churchwoman of today draws from a rich tradition and history. She is studying the history of African Americans and also the history and tradition of Africans, including the religions that count female and male gods among the deities. Her female African American ancestors include slave preachers, free preachers, abolitionists, women's rights advocates, evangelists, church mothers, pastors' wives, pastors, missionaries, deaconesses, writers, Christian educators, social workers, pastors' helpers, businesswomen, lecturers, elocutionists, exhorters, field secretaries, Bible Band workers, and orators. She has high values and high expectations for herself and her church. She has worked hard, and she knows that she has a distinctive witness in her church's mission. No longer content to lead in restricted areas, she has taken on new initiatives and is demanding expanded opportunities for service. She is better informed through ecumenism and has been bombarded with new religious female role models. She approaches both her potential and her barriers more realistically and enthusiastically. She loves the black church and wishes to work more fully on its behalf.

---

[1] Seminary professors who are writing on this topic of "womanist theology" include Dr. Jacquelyn Grant at the Interdenominational Theological Center in Atlanta, Dr. Dolores Williams at the Theological School of Drew University in Madison, N.J., Dr. Kelley Brown Douglas at Howard University School of Divinity, and Prof. Renita Weems at Vanderbilt School of Theology. See Douglas, Weems.

Zipporah

Zipporah, a National Baptist woman, finished her M.Div. degree in 1985, being ordained the same year. She is forty-three years old and single. She became Minister of Education at a 3,500-member church in June 1985. Her total salary package is in the $30,000–$39,000 range. She is located in Alabama in a growing congregation and believes that her M.Div. degree is being fully utilized. She characterizes her acceptance as an ordained minister as being a "gradual process." The region of the country in which she lives is "very conservative and fundamental," but she says, "The longer I stay, the more accepting they are." She observed that there are not many ordained Baptist women in Alabama. On the whole, Zipporah has not been subjected to the stress that other ordained women ministers seeking pastorates experience, because she always wanted to "do education work." She acknowledges that perhaps other women would be frustrated working exclusively in this area, but she is not. By pursuing her ministry in the field of education, Zipporah follows a long tradition of black women who found education to be the only venue in the church open to women's leadership.

Zipporah is not part of a support group, but she does have a trusted mentor, a woman in South Carolina who has founded a church of her own. Her mentor is very supportive of her and frequently invites her to South Carolina. Despite her own nurturing, she has not been a mentor to other women.

Because she is a religious educator, Zipporah rarely modifies her dress. However, she is very aware of the length of her skirt when she sits in the pulpit. On first Sundays, she wears her black clergy robe, and she wears less jewelry when she wears her robe because she thinks that it takes away from her clerical garb. Her interaction with other clergy is limited, except for the ministerial staff of her own church whom she works and socializes with. She describes the male participation in her church as "average," with the men dominating in the more visible leadership roles. Men do not seem to need more encouragement to participate in her church. Zipporah also serves as a chaplain for the National Guard and for a homeless shelter in her city. She spends her leisure time reading, watching movies, and going to plays. Her devotional life consists of Bible study and devotional periods. She would like to enroll in a Doctor of Ministry degree program as a way of improving her ministerial competence, and she has also considered undertaking another degree in education.

Zipporah considers her greatest accomplishment in ministry to be the large educational program of her church. Before she joined the staff, there had not been a large program. She takes pride in the fact that both the people and the church have grown. Indeed, she has grown in her special gifts for ministry in the areas of organization, teaching, Bible studies, and program development. While she is sensitive to inclusive language, she admits that "in a local Baptist church setting, it is very difficult to get people to use it." Her suggestion for enhancing the acceptance of African American clergywomen is to educate clergy and laypeople about sexism and to expose it. In her estimation, the church needs more sensitivity and awareness to the issues of the roles of women in the church. She says, "Those who know should share with those who don't know." Zipporah's experience does reveal a strong male presence in the church and the patriarchal attitudes that come with it. Her church has no problem with male participation, perhaps because in her situation the men hold the most prominent and most visible leadership roles in the church.

Zipporah's source of power comes from her realization that there is a need for clergymen and clergywomen beyond just pastors. She remarks that "not everyone is gifted to pastor." Because of this, she does have to struggle to become other than what she already is. Her favorite image of God is Spirit. For her, God is not male or female, rather God is a presence and power. Her most frequently used theological images are based upon the wisdom of God and the love of God. Zipporah takes comfort in the fact that God is all-knowing and that Christ is primarily a compassionate friend and teacher.

The isolation of black women who minister in specific areas and in certain denominations is highlighted in the case of this woman. She realizes that she has chosen to serve in the arena of education, which has traditionally been more acceptable for women. Zipporah is an example of a woman who has acclimated to the role of an associate within the educational department of a church. The fact that the congregation and its educational program have grown and continue to grow gives her a sense of well-being and accomplishment. She is an example of a woman who has joined the staff of a very large "megachurch" and obviously is meeting the expectations of the church leadership. She is part of a team ministry. Curiously, however, it sounds as if she does not impose high expectations on the people or church to change regarding women in the ministry. Her attitude toward accepting the lack of inclusive language, though it is important to her, shows a resilience and adaptability that many individuals may not be able to display. For her, perhaps the growing health of the congregation is satisfaction enough.

Although she is not pastoring, Zipporah is proud of the strides that women are making in founding and pastoring churches. This is attested to by the selection of her mentor, who founded a church. She is very proud of what this woman has accomplished. Zipporah sees the asset of this mentorship in the fact that this female pastor is very supportive of her and frequently invites her to come to her church. Despite her strong mentor, she longs for more contact with other ordained women, especially those in her own denomination. She testifies to a great need for regional events for black clergywomen that might increase peer support and reach those serving in unlikely places. Zipporah would like to be in touch with seminary-trained women who live in her geographic area, stating, "We don't know each other."

Finally, her passion for education is evidenced by her favorite images of God, with God as the all-knowing source of wisdom. In fact, she stated that there is no separation between the wisdom of God and the love of God. Hers is a special calling within the body of Christ, one that seeks to enlighten Christians as to what is the will of God for their lives through Bible study. Such persons usually stress the moral and ethical dimensions of the faith. Ultimately, Zipporah's most genuine interest is in the growth of the people, emphasizing first that the people have grown, and then that the church has grown.

2

The Ministry as a Profession

Many scholars of American professions count four great professions: law, medicine, ministry, and university teaching. The two central generating qualities of a profession are (1) a basic body of abstract knowledge, and (2) the ideal of service (Etzioni). In a 1972 volume, *The Ministry in Transition,* Yashio Fukuyama traced the use of the word *professional.* It was derived from the adjective "professed," which originally had reference to vows taken by a religious order. The term was secularized in the seventeenth century to refer to the occupation a person professed to follow and be skilled in. The oldest learned professions are law, divinity, and medicine.

In 1961 Howard Becker did a classic study of medical education in *Boys in White.* In this book, he examined student culture while addressing the topic of professional education. He asserted that brief ordeals of initiation, supervised practice, and a long course of professional instruction qualify one for professional status in American society. One must learn what others expect and how they will react to words and actions.

Talcott Parsons described the professional man as one who exercises authority based on superior technical competence. For the ministry, whether priest, pastor, or preacher, these areas have been knowledge of the Bible and theology, leading worship, preaching, and pastoral care. Parsons has described the professional as one who is to a high degree independent of status in kinship groups, the neighborhood and other primary group relationships. The status of the professional is judged on the basis of universalistic criteria determined by one's professional peers and is not subject to the particularism of local groups. Bernard Barber argued that the more professional a profession is, the more likely it is to train its recruits in university-related schools. Such schools have the advantage of transmitting to their students the generalized and systematic knowledge that is the basis of professional performance. In addition, they can borrow resources from other departments, teach, and research cooperatively, sharing university resources (Fukuyama).

In his study of 1,191 pastors and 1,283 seminarians from thirteen seminaries, seven of which were interdenominational, Fukuyama identified three styles of ministry operative within the United Church of Christ, one mainline denomination in America. These styles correspond to three ideal types as theoretical constructions that are the dominant styles of education and ministry. The first is the institutional style, which is oriented toward the denomination. The second is the individualistic style, which is oriented toward the parishioners. The third is the social style, which focuses primarily on the larger community. The institutional style shows a strong commitment to the denomination. The minister's family has been active within a local congregation in the denomination and often he or she has been encouraged to attend a denominational seminary as opposed to an interdenominational one or one affiliated with a university. Such a person enters seminary with a commitment to serve a parish church. He or she typically majors in Bible and theology with a high priority being placed on practical theology. Usually, the student's field education is done in a local church and is positively evaluated. An institutional style minister pursues continuing education in preaching, Christian education, and other practical areas. To such a person, knowledge of denominational structures is considered important. This type of minister is usually conservative on social issues.

The individualistic style of ministry is concerned primarily with parishioners. There is a systematic attempt to gain technical competence in nonreligious fields such as psychology, in addition to the more traditional fields such as Bible and theology. Well-supervised fieldwork and knowledge of the practical field is given high priority. Such a minister is liberal on social issues and only moderately interested in the institutional form of the church. Many of these persons pursue religion and personality majors.

The social style of ministry is most interested in defining the purpose of the church and its ministry. This minister comes from a wider denominational background, and she or he usually comes from a higher socioeconomic status. The social style minister is most critical of institutional forms of the church. In seminary, he or she was not interested in pastoral ministry and has a low commitment to denominationalism while placing a higher value on university-related theological education. She or he is most active on social issues and gives supervised field education low priority. According to Fukuyama, these ministers would rather be college or seminary teachers (Fukuyama).

Pertinent to data in this field are the major findings of Jackson Carroll (1971), whose doctoral dissertation was entitled "Seminaries and Seminarians: A Study of the Professional Socialization of Protestant Clergymen." Carroll found that when the ministers he studied were classified according to their ranking of the goals of theological education during seminary, it was possible to compare four philosophical types on a number of variables. The four types he labeled were: (1) traditional/spiritual, (2) practical/spiritual, (3) traditional/secular, and (4) practical/secular. The traditional/spiritual and practical/spiritual seemed to have had a slightly more religiously grounded preseminary socialization than the traditional/secular or practical/secular. These four types were correlated with three theological school types—the religious community, the vocational school, and the graduate school. Carroll sought to measure the effects of models of theological education on the development of the professional self, which was conceptualized and measured in terms of theological orientation, social-ethical perspective, and image of ministry. The graduate school men were the most liberal theologically, the most contextual ethically, and the most instrumental in their image of ministry. Vocational school graduates tended to fall between the other two types. The more theologically conservative men had less uncertainty over basic issues of faith, while the men who were more liberal theologically tended to be more uncertain. Those who possessed principles oriented toward social issues also tended to adopt more conservative positions on social issues, while contextually oriented men were relatively more liberal. Enjoyment of the more traditional practitioner roles of the minister was positively correlated with an expressive image of ministry and the more contemporary roles with an instrumental image. Theological conservatism, a principles ethical orientation, and an expressive image of ministry suggested a more traditional ministerial stance, while theological liberalism, a contextual ethical perspective, and an instrumental image of ministry seemed to be more contemporary in orientation. Finally, the respondents who were more contemporary in orientation were those who tended to have the greatest problem with professional morale. High morale was positively correlated with the traditional orientation.

The Professional Model of Ministry

According to Carroll (1985), the professional model of ministry has come under critique in recent years. For the sociological critics, the stress on esoteric knowledge and skills is no longer appropriate to describe the essentially sacramental and liturgical tasks of ordained ministry, which have survived the processes of modernization and secularization. Theological critics take aim at several dimensions of professional ministry. One target is its tendency to set the professional ministry apart from the laity, which denies the shared ministry of clergy and laity and creates a dependent laity. They also attack a notion of professional expertise based on functional rationality that reduces ordained ministry to an instrumental, functional capacity to the neglect of its transcendent, sacramental character and the importance of a spiritual call. Finally, the theological-pedagogical critics reject the model as a number of discrete tasks of ministry that are uncritically accepted as what ministry is and what theological education should prepare persons to do.

As a response to this criticism, Carroll attempts to rethink the professional model of ministry. He spells out a new conceptualization of professional clergy who function as reflective practitioners, work interdependently with lay Christians, and model the union of expertise and authenticity, competence and calling, in their being and doing as professional persons (Carroll 1985, 44). Ultimately, Carroll reasserts the importance and significance of a professional model of ministry because the need for full-time clergy leadership will continue. This is especially true among churches peopled by the middle and upper-middle classes among whom modern professionalism developed. There is a valuing of the competence that professionalism implies and a general acceptance of professions as the dominant model for the delivery of essential human services. Although frequently criticized by these class-based groups, the professional model is aspired to by an increasing number of women entering the ministry. Ethnic minorities who are newly entering the middle class and rapidly growing evangelical denominations appealing to lower socioeconomic groups are seeing the most rapid rate of growth. In fact, some of these very groups aspiring to professional status view the criticisms of the professional model as sexist, racist, and classist attempts to undermine professionalization in the ministry just as it has finally become available to them.

This is not to imply that all persons or situations warrant the professional model, or to make it normative for all churches. The model would be dysfunctional for many settings such as Africa, where churches are undergoing explosive growth in membership and where there is a severe shortage of seminary-trained leadership. The model is also dysfunctional in many settings in which the congregation is too small to afford a salaried minister.

One of the greatest strengths of the professional model is its emphasis on competence, which is a primary basis for granting authority to professionals. The kind of competence needed by a reflective ministerial practitioner involves the capacity to act in accordance with an existential knowledge of God and the wisdom of the Christian tradition. The minister is a primary bearer of this tradition who directs attention to particular goals or ends as desirable. As Carroll explains, "The expertise needed is in several broad areas: as meaning definers, as community builders, and as managers of the interface between the church and its social context" (Carroll 1985, 35).

Carroll also calls for the differentiation between professional authority and sacred or charismatic authority, which focuses on the minister's relationship to God. The ordained minister has authority derived from an encounter with the Divine, whether in a dramatic sense of a call to the ministry, or a sense of vocation developed over a period of time through a process of spiritual formation. Carroll wished to absolve the professional model from this domain, while at the same time not de-emphasizing its importance. An Alban Institute study conducted in 1975 reported that laity, when asked to describe factors affecting their relationships with clergy, mentioned most often what John Fletcher labeled "religious authenticity." It was described as "having head and heart together," a clergyperson "who lives the gospel," who is both "a man of God and a man of the world" (Fletcher). Although these two types of authority are analytically and conceptually distinct, Carroll argues for the importance of keeping them together in practice.

Another meaning of calling is set forth by Wilbert E. Moore as being committed in one's profession to "an enduring set of normative and behavioral expectations," involving persistence in the profession, commitment to its norms and standards and loyalty to one's peers (Moore, 5). There is also the service orientation, which can be emphasized as part of the professional model and calling. Understanding one's profession as a calling or vocation includes an expectation that the professional will use his or her expertise responsibly for the good of the community. A calling without professionalization is bumbling, ineffective, and even dangerous. A profession without a calling, however, has no moral and human rootage to keep motivation alive, to keep human sensitivities and sensibilities alert, and to nourish a proper sense of self-fulfillment. Nor does a profession without a calling easily envision the larger ends and purposes of human good that our individual efforts can serve (Gustafson, 514).

The classic work on ministry and educational levels is Liston Pope's *Millhands and Preachers* (1942). His finding was that a denomination lost influence in the cotton mill villages of Gastonia, North Carolina, in rough proportion as its ministerial representatives there became professional religious experts. The Presbyterian Church insisted on theological education for its ministers. The Lutherans did the same. The Methodist ministers had lower educational requirements. Less than one-half had seminary education. College education was not required until 1940. The Baptist ministers had no educational requirement. In 1903, few had high school education; in 1940, only 56 percent had college degrees and only 18 percent had seminary degrees. The leaders of sect groups were almost wholly uneducated, with a fourth- or sixth-grade education, and usually on leave from the mills.

In Pope's study, the Baptists and Methodists had more experience in the immediate conditions of a culture in process of transformation. They were more sensitive to emerging needs and more flexible in adapting their programs to new conditions. As a result, they were more able to interest and lead mill workers. It was difficult securing ministers for the Presbyterian and Lutheran churches. These churches looked for full-time pastors. The Baptist and Methodist churches accepted ministers who worked other full-time jobs. Another of Pope's findings was that theological training was the chief factor in explaining the differences in preaching styles.

If theological training invariably produces upper-class tastes and dispositions, it renders its subjects less socially flexible, while assuming them more competent religiously. If the training is concerned only with religious perspectives and knowledge, its graduates find themselves tremendously disadvantaged in appraising the secular forces that powerfully impinge on their parishes (Pope, 115).

Pope found that, despite years of professional preparation, almost none of the mill pastors had special training in industrial parishes. Their knowledge of economic processes, labor relations, management problems, trade union tactics, and cultural analysis was greatly influenced by their uptown mentality. This led the clergy to isolate themselves from the less educated masses, sharing an uptown view of them as immature, perverse, or inferior. Therefore, it was difficult for the pastors to live at the level of the mill population or to think and speak in terms attractive to mill workers. Most sought to be transferred after a minimum of conscientious service.

Education and the Black Minister

Charles V. Hamilton's book *The Black Preacher in America* (1972) is the most definitive work on the education of black ministers in America. Quoting Dr. Harry Richardson, Hamilton writes, "Recent figures show that only one out of fifteen men entering the ministry has had seminary training" (Hamilton, 412). In other words, 92 percent of black men entering the ministry in 1972 were considered by Hamilton to be professionally unprepared. Reports of conferences of the African Methodist Episcopal Church dating back to before the Civil War are fraught with resolutions calling for more attention to the problem of the lack of formal education among ministers. In spite of this early emphasis on education for ministers, W. A. Daniels, in his work *The Education of Negro Ministers* (1925), reported on a study during the 1920s that found that such training had been inferior to that of other professional departments in black schools. Daniels noted that, contrary to popular belief, men like George Lille, Andrew Bryan, Richard Allen, and others who founded the black church before the Civil War, were men of some education. These were not as educated as the present leaders of the black church, but they were better educated as compared with the laymen of their day than are present leaders as compared with the laymen of his day (Daniels, 89).

This problem that Daniels elucidates has been historically aggravated by two situations: the standards for licensing ministers and the tradition of the "call to ministry." In many denominations the standards for licensing ministers have been lower than those in other professions. In some places, the seminary or theological department has not had the academic prestige comparable to that of other departments or schools. This has proven to be a particular problem in black universities. In the late twentieth century, Lincoln University in Pennsylvania discontinued its seminary altogether. The seminary, under the control of the General Assembly of the Presbyterian Church (USA), was one of the stronger components of the school until after World War II. In the 1950s, it began to acquire a reputation on campus as a place for weaker students. This happened at a time when Lincoln University had achieved a high reputation as a four-year liberal arts college, producing graduates such as Thurgood Marshall, Langston Hughes, and Kwame Nkrumah.

A Baptist deacon in Alabama expressed the issue of the call to ministry taking precedence over education: "I'm not a fighter against education, but education alone will not do the job…We must have a divine call…You can't read enough to be saved" (Hamilton, 91). Rev. W. A. Daniels agreed: "The call to ministry belief…tends to minimize the importance of a high grade theological education and to discount its value" (Daniels, 95). Proving to be equally problematic has been the attitude that some training is better than no training.

In an effort to better train black clergy, theological institutions that remain devoted to training future black preachers have attempted to improve the quality of their education by revising curriculum, increasing libraries, and improving their faculties. One main concern of the African Methodist Episcopal Church has been for a more highly educated ministry that does not sacrifice its commitment to spirituality. However, bishops of the A.M.E. Church expressed concern that members of the church not be educated beyond the general educational level of the ministry. It was felt that this would be detrimental to both the church and the ministry because the parishioners would lose respect for the preachers, thereby under-mining their authority and leading to a decline in membership. According to Hamilton, the fear of followers outstripping the ministry in education had not been a substantial problem. For the most part, congregations either have been satisfied with the educational level of their pastor or the pastor normally has more education than the average layman in the congregation. There is, however, another phenomenon that has occurred in black churches that is the trend among parishioners who achieve a higher education to leave the church of their youth, usually Baptist, to join one of the "high" churches such as Presbyterian, Episcopal, Catholic, or Unitarian. This trend, though disturbing to some, keeps a relative balance between the education of the laity and clergy within the black churches (Hamilton).

Historically, there has been some prestige derived from ministers with college degrees after their names, as there is a fair amount of competition between community churches in this regard. The prevailing attitude was that a pastor with evidence of advanced formal training added increased prestige to a church. This was most noticeable in cities. Writing in the early 1970s, Hamilton described typical small towns and rural black congregations as having educational levels approaching the eighth grade (Hamilton). Hamilton explained that in these congregations it was felt that a seminarian was too educated for their church. "He may come and talk over our heads."

Hamilton concludes that the pastor and pew seek their kind. They are usually not too different from each other educationally. The exception would be the older, self-educated, self-made minister who is at least fifty years old and has maintained strong ties with the families of younger, more educated parishioners. He may have baptized them, buried their parents, or taught them in Sunday school and confirmation. Under such circumstances, these persons usually stay in that less educated minister's congregation.

Although Hamilton's book was written in the 1970s, there was no indication of the existence of black women ministers or seminarians. Like many pulpit studies from this period, black women ministers were elided from the national dialogue on the ministry. This underscores the fact that the 1980s are to be remembered as the decade when the black woman minister comes into visibility within the black church.

Women in Seminary

During the fifties and sixties some seminaries, especially interdenominational ones and those that trained missionaries, allowed women into their Bachelor of Divinity programs (precursor to the M.Div.), typically with the expectation they would teach or work alongside their missionary husbands in foreign lands. The religious music and drama departments of some interdenominational, university-related seminaries also tended to attract women students, as did Christian education programs leading to Master of Religious Education degrees or certificates in a variety of denominational seminaries. Rapidly changing sex distributions in professional degree programs were accompanied by women's demands in the early seventies that seminaries should not only admit more women but also alter their curricular offerings and counseling procedures for women. Especially at the interdenominational, university-associated seminaries in the early seventies, women seminarians pushed for, and typically got, courses as well as other resources (space, funds) devoted to their interests. Courses on "Women in the Church," "Women in the Bible," and the like began to be offered at many schools. Alternative approaches to theological education—such as infusing feminist perspectives on theology and the ministry into courses, support and counseling for women seminarians including dealing with the male establishment in job seeking, advocacy for the use of inclusive language, and hiring of more women faculty— were pursued by women's coalitions inside the seminaries. There was an affirmation of women's right to question and overhaul male-dominated theological perspectives.

The pluralism of the student bodies in university-related schools, their diversity in curricula, and their heritage of theological and social liberalism, predisposed them to accept women into the professional degree program and provide a forum for feminist concerns. Although the number of full-time women faculty in mainline Protestant seminaries has increased very slowly over the last decades, the use of adjunct and part-time women lecturers and tutors has helped increase the number of women faculty.

The study entitled *Women of the Cloth* by Carroll, Hargrove, and Lummis (1983) showed that the great majority of persons who are now parish ministers graduated from denominational seminaries. Only 13 percent of the women and 9 percent of the men got their first professional degrees from one of the interdenominational, university seminaries. While these seminaries have enrolled women, they have not concentrated on training for parish ministry to the same extent as denominational seminaries and are typically not considered by denominational officials as offering as good a preparation for the parish ministry as denominational schools. Although probably a third of these students attending university seminaries will go into and remain in the parish ministry, there may be a difference between students who choose to attend them and those choosing denominational seminaries, as well as differences students may encounter between the schools themselves.

Geographic location was the most frequent reason for choosing to go to a particular seminary, though women slightly more often gave this reason. For example, 22 percent of the women versus 18 percent of the men chose their seminary at least partly because it was near where they or their families lived. Another 20 percent of the women compared with 16 percent of the men chose the seminary because of the area of the country it was in. There were a few denominational differences in the reasons given. At 41 percent, the American Lutheran Church (ALC) women were most likely of all clergy to choose a seminary because it was near home. On average, they are also the youngest clergywomen of all denominations. Forty-three percent of the ALC women compared to 20 percent of the total women were under thirty-one at the time of the study. ALC women were also somewhat more likely to be married, with 63 percent of the ALC women compared to 55 percent of all clergywomen in the study. ALC women as well as men were also more likely than clergy in other denominations to cite a generally popular reason for choice of seminary: The seminary was denominational.

It is clear from the *Women of the Cloth* study that men were considerably more likely than women to have entered seminary because they wanted to be parish ministers, while women were more likely to come to seminary to develop spiritually and find out how they might best use their faith and abilities in the work of the church. Not only were women who eventually became parish ministers more likely to make their decision to enter seminary later and at an older age than men who enter the pastorate, they were also more likely to take longer than men to decide on their ministerial specialty within parish ministry.

While explaining other reasons and motivations for attending seminary, a number of these women further explained that they had couched their ambitions in terms more acceptable for women. The more acceptable reasons and avenues included: pursuing Christian education, theological and intellectual curiosity, and the desire to gain a better understanding of themselves and the faith. A few women indicated they enrolled in the professional degree in order to better assist their minister husbands. After the 50 percent increase in women in seminaries between 1972 and 1974, a higher proportion of women entered seminary with the firm intention of being a parish minister. Women who entered seminary at an older age than the majority were more likely to have had parish ministry as a priority than those who entered young. Some women, in their teens or earlier, develop a conviction that they are called to be pastors and pursue this goal with single-minded devotion. Other women may or may not have decided before they were adults that they wanted to specialize in parish ministry, but probably did look at other forms of ministry and other careers, including marriage and beginning a family. In the course of doing so, they became convinced that they should and could become good pastors and then entered seminary to prepare for this vocation. Although some enter the pastorate after some years as a denominational staff member, chaplain, professor, and the like, the bulk of the remainder will probably, like the women in this study, come to the decision that they want to be pastors as a result of experiences they have in seminary.

The women who began going into professional seminary degree programs in visible numbers in the early 1970s were typically academically superior to their male classmates. There is some indication that this situation led at the time to an alternating, ambivalent treatment of these women seminarians by faculty: valuing them as students, but still uncomfortable with the thought that they might try to be ordained. Most professors were attempting to teach the growing number of women students well. However, it was similarly the case that professors tended to treat male students both in and outside of class as junior colleagues or at least as potentially promising parish ministers if the students were academically above average. They did not, however, appear to be able at that time (with some exceptions) to extend this treatment to academically promising women. Nevertheless, both men and women pastors generally enjoyed their seminary years, though the later women attended seminary, the better they reported that their experiences were. Further, two-thirds of both sexes reported that they have found their seminary education "quite valuable" for their work in parish ministry.

Fully 50 percent of the women pastors who attended university seminaries after 1970 said that they had three or more women professors at their seminaries, compared to only 10 percent of the clergywomen who attended denominational seminaries before 1970. The presence of women professors may indicate why women students at university seminaries had a better chance on the average of being treated seriously as students, though this factor may not necessarily have led faculty to encourage them to be pastors.

It is likely that women seminarians in the 1970s were more open to in-seminary influences than were men. Women were more likely to mention their clergy fieldwork or intern supervisors as quite important influences on their decisions to be ordained (34 percent of the women to 19 percent of the men). They were also more likely to mention other in-seminary or seminary-associated learning experiences that would particularly prepare them for the practice of ministry, such as fieldwork and internships, with 70 percent of the women to 57 percent of the men saying this was quite important in their decisions to be ordained. Also, more women than men said their friends (who were typically classmates in seminary) were quite important in their decision to be ordained. Men, on the other hand, were more inclined to say that the clergy of churches they attended were quite important in their decision to be ordained (51 percent of the men to 40 percent of the women); but for most of the men, this influence came prior to entering seminary. Most women, when they were seminarians, knew no clergywomen (34 percent) or did not know them well enough to obtain modeling clues or even support. As a result, just a third of the clergywomen said that other women pastors were important in their decisions to be ordained. Fortunately, men seem to have learned something from having women around them as fellow seminarians, with many citing the value of continuing collegial relationships with women clergy after ordination.

Motivations for Being Ordained

The most important reason that these clergy, especially women, wanted to be ordained was simply that they felt called by God to ordained ministry. Seventy-seven percent of women, as compared to 67 percent of men, said this was "quite important in their decision to be ordained." Less than 10 percent of these clergy said that such a conviction was unimportant. Also cited as a motivation toward ordination were (1) "a greater acceptance of my ministry by having official church legitimization as an ordained person," and (2) a "desire to administer the sacraments and perform other priestly acts." Both reasons were somewhat more important to women pastors for ordination. For the first statement, 58 percent of the women to 47 percent of the men said this was "quite important." Those questioned also said that ordained status gave them a legitimacy with laypersons, hospital personnel, and others that facilitated their entry into difficult situations as well as their attempts to engage in ministry.

While definitely contributing to opening seminary education and ordained ministry to women, the feminist movement was not the reason that most women gave for entering seminary or the ordained ministry. Once in seminary or the parish, women became more aware of the feminist movement and the degree to which women have been discriminated against within church structures, including the clergy job market and the attitudes of laity and male clergy. Perhaps due to their struggles and lessons learned, women who entered seminary when female enrollment was still small are more likely to have developed a feminist orientation regarding church structures and other aspects of church life.

The history of feminism in denominations and of the responses by churches to the women's movement in the nineteenth and early twentieth centuries are, in one sense, an account of how churches subverted the radical feminist vision of full equality with men into an emphasis on the "special virtue" of women. Beverly Harrison has documented this point forcefully (Harrison).

The emphasis on feminine strengths that women could bring to church organizations and activities tended to lead away from a focus on changing its structures. Such "soft feminists" were often in ideological if not actual conflict with other feminists who stressed androgynous abilities needed for successful performance in occupations. The *Women of the Cloth* study delineated a feminism scale of 1–4, based on responses to the following statements: (1) More women should be ordained to full ministerial status in my denomination. (2) There should be more women in executive staff positions in regional and national offices of my denomination. (3) My congregation should appoint or elect an equal number of laywomen to laymen on the parish governing board. (4) Inclusive language should be used in church publications and services. Less than a third of the women were seeking ordination in order to change the sexist nature of their denominations, though overall this reason was at least somewhat important to about half of the women who became pastors.

Characteristics of Women Seminarians according to Women Faculty

Faculty women most often noted that older women tended to be more dedicated to studying in seminary and becoming pastors than were first-career women. However, the older women were also more likely to be less self-confident about their academic abilities than were the younger women. Older women tended to be much more realistic about life in general and particularly about the parish ministry than most first-career women. This could be because older women seminarians tended to have been actively involved in parishes as laypersons for some years before entering seminary. There also appeared to be a group of second-career women who were coming to seminary more for personal and spiritual "healing" than with the clear vocational goals that were more characteristic of older women students.

Another change among current women seminarians, according to women faculty, was a decrease in women students actively espousing feminist causes and concerns. Most were in agreement that current women students were less aware of, or interested in, women's struggles for recognition and position in church and society historically. Perhaps worse, the students were perceived as lacking any apprehension that they themselves might encounter problems in pursuing an ordained ministry in parishes and chaplaincies because they are women. This may be due to the increase in women students to the point that they are no longer a minority in the student body (or not a small minority), the substantial gains women have made in being accepted and well-treated at seminaries, hearing inclusive language used by most professors and male students, and seeing more women in parish positions. Women were also aware that graduating M.Div. women were getting first parishes with relative ease. Some faculty feared these gains were lulling women seminarians to sleep, assuming the problems of sexism in the ministry to have disappeared.

Dilemmas of Professional Socialization

In 1984, Sherryl Kleinman found that professional schools often transmit messages to their female students that make them feel uncomfortable. She examined the effects on female ministry students in a theology program that promotes an ideology and professional role intended to be inclusive of women. Although the female students valued the ideology, they found it of little use in legitimating themselves to clients, in demonstrating their professional commitment to church hiring committees, or in working out their plans to have a family and a career.

It is during women's years of professional training that a number of experiences crucial to future success take place. For instance, the mentor relationship often has a direct effect on students' later productivity and success (Feldman). Male teachers and peers sometimes question female students about how they will juggle family and career involvements, thereby challenging the women's future commitment to their careers (e.g., Bourne and Wikler, Hammond, Podmore and Spencer).

In most professional schools today, women are a distinct minority. In addition to suffering the problems of being tokens in a male-dominated environment (Kanter), female students may receive messages that are male oriented. There are expectations of all professionals to fit conventional expectations of men. The male professional is expected to act authoritatively and to be effectively neutral. He is supposed to be distant (personable but not personal) and elitist, conveying the idea that as a professional, he knows how to solve his clients' problems better than they do (Hughes). Female professional students feel uncomfortable with these expectations (Epstein, 73).

As a father to his parishioners, the minister has traditionally played the role of knowing counselor and moral exemplar. The parishioners, on the other hand, look to the minister for comfort and guidance, viewing him as a human being with superhuman knowledge and power (Schuller, Brekke, and Strommen, 73). The minister's image, in other words, is dependent on his maintenance of a traditionally masculine stance in relation to his parishioners.

The Kleinman study looked at a professional theology program of three hundred students, nearly one-third of whom were female. The program offered an ideology intended to "humanize" the professional-client relationship. Although the ideology protected the women in their daily interactions in the seminary, they found it of little use in legitimating themselves to clients, in demonstrating their professional commitment, or in handling their future problems of having both a family and career. The female students learned that most parishioners see "woman" and "minister" as contradictory statuses (Charlton). One way they talked about this problem was by complaining that they had not had a role model. Many of the women had never seen, let alone known, a female minister. Others regarded the female role and the ministerial role as contradictory. Several of the women reported that others said they should become ministers' wives rather than ministers.

In this study, humanistic ideology undercut their full and effective participation as ministers. For example, the toleration implied in humanism made it difficult for many women to take a stand against others' use of sexist language. The students' ambivalence toward humanism could also be seen in their negative assessment of female faculty and courses especially designed for women. Of the three female faculty members, the women preferred the one they described as "more human," more interested in people. They liked one of the others, but felt that the third was too intellectually oriented, too unconcerned with interpersonal relations, and acted like a man.

These data indicate that the female students accepted the humanization role. The students felt that a woman's course should be experiential but should also provide intellectual, theological justification for women's participation in the ministry and for feminist or innovative worship. The women largely endorsed humanism because it is an ideology that legitimates their place in the ministry and a perspective they value. They had some sense, however, that parishioners would define an extreme humanistic orientation as not only unconventional (and hence illegitimate) but also feminine. Fully accepting the humanistic role was tantamount to accepting conventionally adopted feminine, and hence conventionally less authoritative, behaviors.

If Sennett is correct in asserting that people today value personalized work relations, clients may view the male who acts humanistically as having the most acceptable professional style—he is not only competent and professionally authoritative but human and caring as well. On the other hand, parishioners may regard a woman who uses the humanistic language as simply doing what comes naturally; they may view her as caring, but she may not be accepted as competent. In the eyes of parishioners, female ministers cannot prove they are competent by appealing to an ideology that delegitimates authority generally and calls for acting and thinking in ways conventionally associated with femininity.

Most professional women have problems juggling the responsibilities of family and career. Some professions are organized in ways that make it extremely difficult for women to have conventional family lives and careers. The military, the business world, academia (to some extent), and certain denominations of the ministry expect their employees to move often and to wherever the company sends them. As Kleinman discovered, the Methodist ministry is organized in this appointment way and therefore poses problems for many women. Once accepted for ordination by a conference, ministers are guaranteed church employment. In return for this guarantee they must accept appointment wherever the bishop places them. In addition, Methodists hold to a system of itinerancy; Methodist ministers change churches frequently, on average, every four years. In light of this system, male ministers with professional wives should have the same problems that female ministers with professionally committed husbands have. But since more wives who have professional training move to their husband's place of employment than the reverse (Feldman, and Wallston, Foster, and

Berger), female students are likely to have a bigger problem than their male colleagues. In addition, since women retain the major responsibility for housekeeping and childcare (Pleck), female ministers who plan to have children may also anticipate major problems. It is not surprising, then, that the *Women of the Cloth* study found that only 55 percent of female pastors compared with 94 percent of male pastors were married.

Because it is egalitarian and inclusive, the humanistic ideology allows women to believe that their profession is largely meritocratic and nondiscriminating. They believe that as long as they work hard, the church will offer them the same rewards given to hard-working male ministers. This belief is functional in the short run, for it makes it easier for the women to work hard in meeting the demands of their programs without worrying about the possibly sexist questions of church committees. At the same time, it keeps them from strategizing and dealing head-on with future professional problems.

Most of the women assumed that it would be their responsibility, not the man's, to juggle career and home life. This suggests that though these women were not radical, they were not naive. Rather, the women used the ideology to make realistic accommodations to their inequitable situations. Actually the ideology had a boomerang effect for some women who faced the conflict. Nearing ordination or graduation, some of the women panicked in anticipation of the problems of having both a conventional family life and a career and actually used the inclusive ideology to question their own commitments to the ministry and even to exit their programs. Some talked about how they might minister as mothers and wives. Here they demonstrated the humanistic emphasis on inclusiveness in ministry. Other women noted that once they became ministers, men might not be attracted to them, suggesting that people who do accept the woman as minister (i.e., as someone in authority) also cannot accept that minister as a woman. A couple of the women in Kleinman's study who contemplated leaving the program were among the most actively involved in the life of the school, were doing well academically, and were regarded by other students and teachers as persons who would make good ministers. In dealing with their conflicts, they suddenly developed what appears to be the will to fail (Horner). Thus, the ideology made the women vulnerable in unintended ways when they had to face male bias in the occupational structure and in expectations for gender roles in marriage. Kleinman concludes her article by making the point that the socialization process in professional schools cannot help women solve their problems in professional careers until gender expectation and the structure of professional work are changed.

The seminary organized itself around several academic disciplines, using the university model of education claiming objectivity as the rationale for a supposedly value-free approach to scholarship. The Cornwall Collective, a project of the Auburn History Project, which was funded by the Lilly Endowment, challenged this premise and described the seminary model as hierarchical, competitive, and heavily weighted with class, race, and gender bias. The book *Your Daughters Shall Prophesy* describes the activities of women's groups that have been established within seminaries throughout the country to advocate change, which will make theological education more responsive to the needs and interests of women, both students and faculty. As newcomers to the seminaries, women are acutely conscious of the importance of who shapes the dialogue and determines the criteria for who and what is included as a valid part of the educational experience.

Nancy Hardesty sets forth the theory that the relationship between women and seminaries seems to evolve through four stages. During the first stage, few women are present. They are grateful for the opportunity to study at the seminary. They hope to find some form of ministry on the fringes of the church to satisfy the inescapable call of God they feel in their hearts. Male students, unthreatened, are friendly and patronizing. Male faculty is solicitously paternal. During stage two, as small groups of women gather in a seminary context, their consciousness is raised. They get in touch with sexism in church and society and with their own anger. They form an embattled women's caucus, knowing that the skirmishes they fight in seminary are preliminary rounds for the battles they will fight for their right to full ministry in the church. Their stance evokes hostility from their male peers. There is resistance from the faculty. The women's demands are met by concessions. During stage three, as more women students arrive, the fervor of women and the fever of the situation dissipates. Changes are made. Several women are hired on the faculty, a few feminist theology or women-in-ministry courses are added to the curriculum. New women students wonder what the problem is. Younger ones have encountered few difficulties thus far in their education or church experience. They have seen female role models in the parish, and they see themselves as being no different from their male peers. They compare notes on church politics and plan for their own parishes. Faculty and student men have learned to speak "nonsexist," and so a modicum of harmony reigns. During the fourth stage, women come to appreciate past struggles and gains while being realistic about the depths of prejudice and the difficulties remaining. Women faculty are no longer marginal but integral to the faculty. An awareness of feminist, black, and liberation theologies informs the critique of all theology and biblical hermeneutics (Hardesty).

During most of the history of theological education, theology has only been taught and learned as structured by white, European scholars. Throughout those years, the black experience of oppression was not a serious object of theological reflection. Nor did its reality help define the theological task in terms supportive of justice and equality for black people. J. Deotis Roberts (1969), in an essay entitled "The Black Caucus and the Failure of Christian Theology," analyzed the black caucus trend in white churches as a theological issue. According to James Cone, white theology minimized the social determination of theological knowledge by appealing to the Bible, divine revelation, or a common humanity. Cone, himself a leading proponent of black theology, insists that "one's praxis in life inevitably shapes one's theological perceptions" (Cone and Wilmore, 139). He further premises that the oppression of black people can be a point of departure for analyzing God's activity in contemporary America.

J. Deotis Roberts' writing "The Hermeneutic Circle of Black Theology" (1983) explains that liberation theology, like black theology, starts from the present realities and looks backward. For black theology, racism is a theological problem because God creates all persons, and God gives racial characteristics. To value one group above another is to choose the judgment of the creature over that of the Creator who made human beings in the Creator's image.

The literature on black theology is voluminous. It comprises what has been written not only in the United States but also in Africa and the Caribbean. It has earned its rightful place in the theological curriculum. The same is true of feminist theology. Church history courses include material about all segments of church life—clerical and lay, white and black, men and women, bishops and Sunday schools, General Conference decisions and the work of the Women's Foreign Missionary Society. Men and women choose, and the church affirms forms of ministry for which the individual persons are gifted, whether parish work or more specialized endeavors. Couples find support for flexible solutions to the complex issues raised by equalitarian marriages and family rearing.

Women in Ministry

Very little quantifiable or qualitative data is available on women in ministry. Much work is currently in progress and being published. Although it is an important area of professional leadership around the world, its impact has yet to be fully ascertained. While women's working in other professions is increasingly acceptable, the ministry is viewed as different. Suzanne Hewitt, writing about women priests in the Episcopal Church in 1973, attributed this attitude to the following: (1) the reverence for male priests as keepers of mysteries, (2) the nostalgia for the Victorian church and the "good old days," (3) adherence to patriarchy as the "proper" way to organize society (Hewitt and Hiatt).

As a result of patriarchal society, many women tend to view life as men wish them to view it, creating female attitudes that are apt to be derivative of male attitudes. Men presently control the church's policy and practice, and it is, therefore, men who still prevent and delay fuller participation by women in the church. This refutes a commonly held notion that women in the church are the greatest opponents to women in ministry. In fact, part of a larger study of several denominations in two different cities, entitled the "Women in Transition Project" (WIT), found that among twelve United Methodist Churches studied, six had women pastors and one had a female assistant pastor. In those churches where women had leadership, the participation of women active in the congregation was greater than in other cases. One of the conclusions of the in-depth study was that a female pastor seems to encourage women to seek help more readily and for a wider range of concerns (Van Scoyoc).

Reverend Karen Smith Sellers, a United Church of Christ minister, reminded her readers that the minister has traditionally been a cultural hero, an ideal type who exemplifies moral and religious values. She pointed out that women, apart from the image of the Virgin Mary, which Protestant women rarely emulate, do not have positive religious images. More often, women are thought of according to the image of Eve, who seduced Adam and led to man's downfall (Sellers). Another problem that women encounter, apart from exemplifying the holy, is the stereotype that women are only passive and submissive. The prevailing stereotype of the minister, on the other hand, is as one who leads with assurance and preaches with authority.

In January 1979, 650 United Methodist women ministers and seminarians met in Dallas, Texas, at Southern Methodist University. Full ordination had been granted United Methodist women in 1956. Only in the seventies had women entered the ministry in appreciable numbers. By 1979, the denomination had 766 women serving under appointment as ministers and several hundred in seminary. According to Jean Coffey Lyles, "appointability" was a key word used against women's placement and whether single, married to another minister, or married to a nonclergy professional, women were regarded in the church hierarchy as "difficult to place" (Lyles). When bishops have had the courage to appoint women to pastoral slots, congregations have typically accepted them warmly. According to Lyles, most women say their chief problem is not lack of acceptance by laity, but the hostility of male pastors who feel threatened by competition in a job market with little room at the top. While most other Protestant denominations operate under a "call" organization, with each congregation hiring and firing pastors on its own, under United Methodism's itinerant plan, ministers are appointed to pastoral charges by the bishop. The unemployment problem plaguing clergy in other denominations is minimized, for every fully credentialed pastor is guaranteed an appointment. Of course, this means accepting the bishop's authority to determine where one will serve, and being willing to go where one is sent. In this system, the ultimate goal in upward mobility is episcopacy. A Michigan woman urged then District Superintendent Marjorie Matthews to stand for election, and Matthews was eventually elected bishop. Bishop Matthews had a reputation as an establishmentarian and staunch defender of itinerancy. She also had a reputation for being supportive of women who were more radical than she. Speaking to The United Methodist Church, she wrote, "Open itinerancy is seldom a reality; few women pastors are appointed to churches of more than 300 members except in associate slots; almost never has a woman served as senior pastor in a multiple staff situation" (Lyles, 117). In 1983, The United Methodist Church elected its first black woman bishop.

Turning to the United Church of Christ (UCC), which operates under the "call" organization, Sellers reports 452 women ordained clergy in 1979. In a survey, almost 100 percent of the UCC women ministers indicated that they felt discrimination from pastoral search committees. Two-thirds said they experienced acceptance and support once hired (Sellers). In spite of this, the women suffered internal ambiguity, had trouble planning life goals, had difficulty writing compelling and convincing dossiers, and were unsuccessful at using placement systems. In spite of this fact, Sellers concluded that women bring fresh questions, perceptions, and concerns to the ministry. They seek new ways of integrating their personal and professional lives, working in unfamiliar contexts, and trying new things, such as alternate sources of religious authority and new names for God. Sellers stated, "The Church is slow to change. It is not bound by state or federal laws regarding affirmative action or civil rights...Equal opportunity for women will come about by the slow methods of education and persuasion" (Sellers, 18). Another UCC minister stated, "The congregation has just gotten over its grief: the grief they felt at having sunk so low in the company of parishes that it had been forced to hire a woman as pastor rather than a 'real' minister, i.e., a man" (Hiatt, 124).

In 1972 the Department of Ministry and Worship of the Christian Church (Disciples of Christ) engaged the services of a consultant in Women's Ministries for the purpose of validating some impressions regarding the employment of women in positions of professional church leadership and to assist the department in formulating programs of enlistment, education, and utilization. The study found that in a day when science, education, business, and industry continued to open new doors of opportunity to women, the Christian Church (Disciples of Christ) was slowly diminishing the number of women it employed from 288 in 1962 to 189 in 1972.

Forty percent of the women listed in the 1972 "Ministers Directory of the Year Book" responded to an extensive questionnaire. The survey suggested that 88 percent had at least a bachelor's degree and 63 percent had earned a graduate degree. Seventy-six percent were ordained. The average salary was $6,500 per year. The majority of the respondents were in the thirty-six to fifty age bracket and had other types of employment before preparing to enter the ministry. In light of this delay, two problems stood out. While 64 percent of the women employed in the church in 1972 were directors of Christian education, only 25 percent really preferred that as a form of ministry. Conversely, while only 5 percent were pastors, 20 percent would have liked to be. If one agrees that people are most productive when they are doing what they really want to do, then it follows that the church was failing to get the maximum potential from a large

number of its ministers. Frequently, these women stated that they
felt they were not taken seriously, were overlooked, and were
underpaid. They were told that the ministry is man's work, that they
ought to find a husband, and that they should "prove themselves."
Yet 83 percent affirmed that in spite of these obstacles they would
do it again. The majority agreed that young girls should be
encouraged to prepare for Christian ministry.

Regarding career goals, 35 percent of those surveyed would
choose pastoral ministry, 25 percent pastoral counseling, 14 percent
Christian education, 14 percent higher education, including seminary
teaching, and 9 percent regional ministries. However, these young
women had obstacles. They cited that they frequently were not taken
seriously, had difficulty in earning a living and studying, and found
few positions open to them. One summed up her frustrations this
way: "It is difficult to be a single woman trying to find a place in a
family-oriented occupation." The respondents were aware that as
women, their salaries would not likely be the same as those offered
to men with the same training and ability, and they wondered why.
They knew that changing attitudes toward the employment of women
is a slow process but felt that an effort should be made to make
successful women more visible in the churches. They heard that
many men clergy were not ready to accept women as associates,
sharing all pastoral responsibilities. They knew that as women they
had to be highly qualified. These women expressed their need "to
see models; we need to meet women in consultation who can
explicitly acquaint us with problems to be faced and enable us to
articulate ours." The report recommended that laywomen
undoubtedly can do much to change attitudes by urging the
employment of women in all areas of ministry. More help was needed
from the regional and general units of the church in making known
that there are well-trained women available for employment.

In 1983, *Women of the Cloth* was the first baseline, sociological
study written on clergywomen in the United States. It was made
possible by a generous grant from the Ford Foundation and assistance from Hartford Seminary and Iliff School of Theology. Nine
denominations also assisted with this study. The *Women of the Cloth*
study (WOC) conducted hour-long telephone interviews with 636
clergywomen randomly selected from the following denominations:
(1) American Baptist, (2) American Lutheran, (3) Christian Church
(Disciples of Christ), (4) Episcopal Church, (5) United Church of
Christ, (6) United Methodist, (7) Lutheran Church in America,

(8) Presbyterian Church (USA), and (9) United Presbyterian Church in the USA. Prior to the telephone call, they each received a letter from the researchers and a letter from an official in their denomination. The women were then compared to a random sample of men from the same denominations. All data that follows in this chapter comes from that study.

Table 1 compares the status of women in the ministry to other professions.

TABLE 1
Numbers and Percentages of Women in Selected Professions
(Jacquet, 5; Bureau of Labor Statistics)

	Clergy		Lawyers/Judges		Physicians	
	No.	%	No.	%	No.	%
1930	3,276	2.2	3,385	2.1	6,825	4.6
1940	3,148	2.3	4,187	2.4	7,608	4.6
1950	6,777	4.1	6,256	3.5	11,714	6.1
1960	4,272	2.3	7,543	3.5	16,150	7.0
1970	6,314	2.9	13,406	4.9	26,084	9.3
1980	11,130	4.2	70,106	12.8	46,008	10.8

The fifty-year figures show an increase of 240 percent in the overall number of women clergy. In spite of this, compared to law and medicine, the percentage of women is relatively small. It is clear that the ministry is still male dominated, as are the other two professions. Women in all three professions made their greatest gains in the seventies, though ministry lagged far behind law.

The *Women of the Cloth* study found that women clergy tended to come from higher-status backgrounds than men clergy. Having a father who pursued a professional or business career seemed an important factor for these women. While the ministry is seen as a path toward social mobility for the sons of lower-middle-class and working-class families, daughters are actively discouraged due to the perceived lack of opportunities, the tendency for lower classes to be more theologically fundamentalist in orientation to the Bible, and preconceived notions concerning women's place in religious leadership (Barfoot and Sheppard). This does not mean that most clergywomen come from high social class backgrounds. One-half of the clergywomen had fathers who were business executives, clergy, or other professionals. Between one-fourth and one-third came from the working class. For those women who were ordained in 1975 and after, 12 percent had clergy fathers. Table 2 shows the occupations of father and mother in the *Women of the Cloth* study. The predominant pattern of these clergywomen was one of consistent and active religious socialization. Sixty-nine percent were ordained in the denomination in which they were raised.

As one can see in Table 2, 44 percent of the clergywomen had mothers who worked outside the home. Why these women chose the ministry over other professional careers, such as medicine or law, may lie partially in the fact that they were typically raised in families where at least one of the parents was active in a church when they were growing up. Clergy who were more active in a church during their college years were more likely to make an early decision to enter the ministry. Overall, women were more likely to make a later decision than men to enter seminary.

Among those parish ministers who worked full-time prior to ordination, the women who worked outside the home were in higher status occupations than men who worked prior to ordination. Most often these women were teachers, nurses, social workers, librarians, and secretaries. More women than men came into the ministry as a second career.

TABLE 2
Occupations of Women Clergy's Mothers and Fathers
(Carroll, Hargrove, and Lummis, 54)

	Father's Occupation	Mother's Occupation
Clergy, Business Executive, Professional	41%	17%
Middle Management	22%	8%
Clerical	9%	16%
Blue Collar	27%	5%
Not in Labor Force (Housewife, Retired, Unemployed)	1%	56%

Women Clergy in the Job Market

Regional judicatory officials were usually crucial in the success or failure that women clergy met in the job market. Eighty-five percent of the women were able to find a position within six months; 91 percent found positions within a year. Consequently, the *Women of the Cloth* study concluded that the problem was not with entry-level jobs, but rather with second, third, and subsequent placements. It should be kept in mind that *Women of the Cloth* only surveyed those women who were already in the parish. It did not factor in those women who may have wanted a parish position and never found one.

Lehman's American Baptist data indicates that the greater the number of formal structures used by a woman, the more her formal identity as a minister is likely to be legitimated (Lehman 1979). In Lehman's study of Presbyterian women, the findings were similar to those for American Baptist women. Lehman documented how the number of "special needs" restricts chances for satisfactory placement and salary level for the candidates. To define special needs, respondents were given a list of factors that might limit the location and nature of a church job. They included such restrictions as their spouse's jobs, their children's needs, and their educational needs. The greater the number of needs specified, the fewer the number of interviews the candidate had, the fewer the calls she received, and the lower her salary (Lehman 1981).

While 88 percent of the men in *Women of the Cloth* were in sole or senior pastor positions, women were significantly more likely to be assistant or associate pastors and were less likely to be sole or senior pastors of churches. Women may be choosing assistant and associate positions because better salaries are attached to them. Often these positions are located in large towns and cities where there are more opportunities for support and interaction with congenial persons outside the parish. Although the study was cross-sectional and not longitudinal, it appeared that women were more likely than men to enter the ministry in assistant and associate positions and remain there. Six out of ten women enter in assistant or associate pastor roles; four out of ten in a third or more positions are at the same level. Men, on the other hand, progressively move to sole or senior pastor positions. Twenty-five percent of the women and 5 percent of the men were part-time pastors, with most working half or three-fourths time. A large number of the part-timers were married to another clergyperson.

Clergywomen were significantly less likely than men (48 percent to 63 percent) to describe the dominant theological position of each one's congregation as very or moderately conservative. Liberal churches are more likely to be open to women. There was a greater congruence of theological position perceived by males concerning their own and their congregation's stance, as compared with women clergy. A slight majority of both sexes, but more clergywomen, considered their positions to be more liberal, with 69 percent women to 51 percent men. Both clergywomen and men were equally as likely to say that their churches were declining when they arrived (46 percent women and 44 percent men); that they were located in a small city, small town, or rural area (both 80 percent); that their churches were predominately middle and upper class (54 percent women and 56 percent men); and that the present financial health was excellent or good (40 percent women and 46 percent men). Women were more likely to be in churches of fewer than 200 members, and 9 percent of women stated that they were in churches where two-thirds of the members were age 50 and older. The hypothesis that women are more likely to be called to declining churches was not supported.

There were strong and significant differences between women and men in their second, third, or more parishes. The third or more parishes of women were more likely than men to be located in small cities, small towns, or rural areas and to have older members. Both second and third parishes of women were more likely to be small (under 200 members), have fewer middle- and upper-class members, and less likely to be in good or excellent financial health. Thus, women who were sole or senior pastors did not appear to keep pace with clergymen in the kinds of positions to which they were called or appointed over the length of their careers.

Overall, 39 percent of clergywomen as compared with 10 percent of the clergymen received a salary of less than $10,000, though some of this difference might be reflected in the considerable difference in experience. Comparing women and men with five or less years of experience, the salary difference remained. While 16 percent of the men earned less than $10,000, 40 percent of the women did. Part-time employment counted for some of the differential. Twenty-seven percent of women working full-time earned $10,000, and only 7 percent of the men working full-time did so. The number of years of experience in ministry plays a small, but statistically significant, positive role. Being part-time had the most significant negative effect on salary. For men more than women, years of experience increased the chances for a higher salary, as Carroll, Hargrove, and Lummis remarked in 1983: "Evidently the doctrine of equal pay for equal work is not any more observed by many churches than by other institutions" (Carroll, Hargrove, Lummis, 132). In spite of salary differences, women were more likely than men to say that they usually had sufficient money during the last year to live comfortably (72 percent of women to 61 percent of men).

The use of inclusive language was greatly advocated by clergywomen. Agreeing with the item "Inclusive language should be used in all church publications and services" were 88 percent of the clergywomen and 53 percent of clergymen. While the use of inclusive language was highly important to them personally, a number of the women indicated that they would take care in how they introduced it into their worship services, not forcing it on their congregations.

Clergy Couples

Thirty-one percent of the clergywomen surveyed in the *Women of the Cloth* study were married to ordained clergymen. This compares with 2.5 percent of the clergymen who were married to ordained clergywomen. Women were much more likely to have married during seminary. Most clergymen surveyed were in the ministry longer and finished seminary before the large influx of women. Of the 55 percent of clergywomen who were married, almost two-thirds were married to an ordained minister. Because the placement of ordained couples involves securing two jobs rather than one (or a shared job), and because two careers do not always run on the same track or at equal speeds, an early decision has to be made relative to whose career goals will take priority. The most popular option seemed to be functioning in the same parish. Fifty-seven percent of the women and 72 percent of the men work in the same parish with their spouse. One-third of the women and one-fifth of the men work in different parishes from their spouses, with fewer than 10 percent indicating that their spouses were in nonparish work settings. Clergywomen were more likely to be part-time. This arrangement may be seen as acceptable because laity may be transferring to the women the additional expectations of the pastor's wife. In many cases, pastors' wives have functioned or been expected to function as unpaid assistant ministers. In cash salary, women and men who are part of a clergy couple are somewhat more likely to report making less salary than other clergy. Only 21 percent of men married to an ordained woman reported making over $15,000, as compared to 51 percent of the total sample of men.

Ruth

Ruth, an Episcopal woman, was ordained to the diaconate in 1987 and to the priesthood in 1989. She is single and serving a 135-member parish that is growing. Uncharacteristically, all three Episcopal churches in her area are led by women. Currently, Ruth does not feel that she is fully using what she learned in seminary because her church is small and she is overtaxed by doing everything in the church except the duties of the sexton and organist. Because she has to perform nonclergy functions, Ruth does not have time to use all the skills that she acquired in seminary. Her greatest opportunity for ministry has been in the area of healing ministry. Several years ago, Ruth began the laying-on-of-hands during service and found that many people came forward to participate. Ironically, she has found the men in her congregation to be most accepting of her ministry. Although they were a little standoffish at first, when they saw that she was doing a good job, they accepted her. She feels that sometimes it is difficult for women to accept a woman in authority, as a leader, stating, "They seem rather competitive with me." While Ruth feels that men need more encouragement than women to participate in the church, she has found the men to be "very, very cooperative. They do as much as they can do. They try to be supportive. They do what I ask them to do; often they volunteer without my asking them."

When asked what the difference is between black female M.Div. graduates and black male M.Div. graduates, she said that men have more opportunities. She remarks, "Women are doers. They go out of their way to impress the male pastors. That makes a difference." A male priest preceded Ruth, and she is the first female priest at the parish. Curiously, her male predecessor had a woman who volunteered as his secretary, but Ruth does not. When asked why she cannot get a volunteer to do the same for her, she said, "They see that I can do a lot, and they figure, 'Let her do it.' Not having a secretary has been a problem. That has slowed me down."

Ruth is part of an Episcopal clergy support group that is headed by a male minister. For the first seven months in her geographic area she had a mentor, but not now. She has not directly mentored other women.

With regard to her clerical appearance, she has never worn fingernail polish or much makeup. This has not changed. Since she serves communion every Sunday and must place the elements in persons' mouths, she does not feel that fingernail polish would be appropriate. She is careful to appropriately cleanse her hands because of the way in which she must handle the sacraments. For the most part, she wears an alb and chasuble.

Serving on her church's board, Ruth interacts with other clergy in her area through the monthly meeting of a Ministerial Alliance. She also serves on the boards of three community service organizations. In her leisure, Ruth takes piano lessons and plays the piano, but mainly she rests, saying, "It takes a lot of vitality to be a parish priest." Eventually, Ruth would like to gain greater competency in biblical studies. Her greatest accomplishment thus far in ministry has been leading this small parish. She has used her organizational skills to foster persons to follow. She considers preaching her greatest gift for ministry. She said, "I'm lagging behind time on inclusive language. It doesn't bother me to say 'Father' and 'his,'" but adds, "I try to make my language inclusive because others are sensitive to male-dominated language."

To improve the visibility of black women in the ministry, Ruth suggests that women ministers need to go to school career days to let the girls know that they exist and to help the girls see examples of what they can become. Her source of power is prayer, and her favorite image of God is Shepherd. Her most used image for God is as Holy Spirit. The attributes that she uses most for Christ are Healer and Counselor. Her favorite image for Christ is Savior.

Ruth's case is remarkable in terms of the strong bonding that she seems to feel toward the male parishioners. Unfortunately, there appears to be some competition between her and the laywomen, and she does not find the women to be as helpful as she would like. Because religion is highly feminized, women fulfill most of the functions necessary to keep the day-to-day operations of the church going. In a sense the entrance of a paid clergywoman often upsets the "sexual politics" of the church. Laywomen in the black church often receive their greatest affirmation from the male clergy who represent power and authority. Although it is undeniable that the male has traditionally represented both sacred and secular authority, both clergywomen and clergymen represent the presence and compassion of God in a special way. Why this is not sufficient to engender respect and authority in this woman's case is unknown.

With regard to women ministers having to do secretarial work, this again is evidence of a strong cultural bias. Most secretaries are women, and most educated women are expected to type and do clerical tasks. Many churches often have a number of retired women who have previously been secretaries and who may choose to serve as administrative aides in the church on a volunteer basis. In Ruth's case, these women did not find it necessary to assist her in this way. Another problem that churches face is the aging of its population. Important to consider is that younger clergywomen often come to the church with computer skills that might intimidate the older women. However, with training and encouragement for a number of them to purchase computers, these women can become very excited about acquiring this new skill. In my own church, there are now two older women who are proud of how they can be productive on the computer on behalf of the church. This is one area where younger members, especially youth, could teach the elderly how to use new technologies, including the Internet. It can be a great blessing to so many who cannot move around as freely as they once did.

Ruth reminds us of the high energy level that is required to lead a congregation. It can be physically demanding and exhausting. Many older church buildings are themselves obstacle courses in which to move around. Many days I feel as if I need roller skates in order to cover the now four buildings that make up our complex. Although they are all connected into one, there are many steps, twists, and turns in our building. Trying to find the appropriate individuals throughout the day demands intercoms, beepers, and portable phones. Add home and hospital visitation, hanging out with the youth groups, and attending myriad activities that various groups within the church sponsor, and you get the picture of how much sheer physical exertion is involved.

Youthful energy is certainly an asset in these cases. Many times you must host fellowship events. As pastor it requires either a large family to help you or trusted friends and congregants who pitch in and help.

Ruth's healing ministry is one that is being actively recaptured by men and women of the cloth. At one time the laying-on-of-hands was very popular, but it was pushed aside in our secularized church culture. Today many clergy are finding this a powerful liturgy of touch and connection with the hurts of families and individuals. I call healing ministries "radical love." It says, "Give me your hurts, diseases, concerns, and burdens for a minute while I lay hands on you. I will stand in the gap and go to God on your behalf in a very personal, intimate way." The Spirit moves mightily in healing services, and grace is experienced in special ways. I used to confine my own anointing services to private sessions within the context of counseling. Then I started anointing parishioners with oil twice a year in the chapel. Now we have moved this activity to a monthly healing ministry in the main sanctuary immediately following morning worship. This has been very successful; there is always some compelling situation that warrants intense prayer sessions like these. Sometimes it is a person from the community who requests the anointing, or sometimes it is a family or member of the church. At Michigan Park Christian Church, we have started a study group on the subject among the ten ministers. We will then open it to our elders and finally take it in to one of the five weekly adult Bible classes.

Some ministers feel uncomfortable with anointing and should not undertake it. This is all right. However, other ministers find it to be quite effective. My experience is that many Christians desire anointing, and I always make it voluntary, so that all those who participate genuinely appreciate it. In this tradition, once a year I ask all health workers and professionals, including those who are retired, to help with the healing and anointing prayer services. Usually the medical doctors and nurses are more than happy to assist. I think that lay deacons and elders should be trained to extend this ministry to parishioners on request or as the Spirit moves. Some pastors who do not feel comfortable doing this can invite other ministers to come in and train their leaders in this ministry. It is also a good idea that, in the context of traditional black church revivals, a healing ministry may be manifested. As we know, Jesus is the great Physician. It is interesting that Ruth, who is involved in the healing ministry, cited Healer as one of her favorite attributes of Christ. It appears that the clergy in this study are drawn to images and attributes of God and Christ that resonate with the movement of the Holy Spirit in their own personal and priestly experiences.

3

The Professionalization of
the Ministry of Black Women

This chapter will focus on some of the findings of a national survey of black female Master of Divinity (M.Div.) graduates who finished seminary between 1972 and 1984. Using data reported in the *Fact Book on Theological Education,* table 3 shows the M.Div. enrollment of all women and of black women (Taylor). In the interval reported, the enrollment of black men increased by 123.6 percent and of black women by 676.1 percent. Proportionately, black women kept up with and surpassed all women in the professional degree during this period. In 1983–1984, women accounted for 17 percent

TABLE 3
Numbers and Percentages of Women Enrolled in M.Div. Programs

Year	Number of Women	Percentage of Students	Number of Black Women	Percentage of All Blacks
1973	1077	4.7	34	5.0
1976	2544	9.3	87	8.8
1979	3981	12.6	170	12.4
1982	5286	16.0	288	16.9
1983	5607	16.6	354	19.6
1984	6009	17.0	399	20.0

of M.Div. enrollment. Black women accounted for 20 percent of black enrollment.

To ascertain whether or not there were sufficient numbers of black female M.Div. graduates to justify the type of research designed, some projected figures were formulated. The *Fact Book* does not publish data on black female M.Div. completions. But based upon an average completion rate of 17 percent reported for blacks during select years, and using the percentages of black female enrollments, it was estimated that there were approximately 368 black female M.Div. graduates between 1972 and 1984.

Dr. Marvin Taylor, for years the editor of the *Fact Book,* checked ninety-three schools from the listing of member institutions that could have graduated black female M.Div. students. Dr. Lawrence Jones, Dean Emeritus of Howard University Divinity School, wrote a cover letter urging each seminary executive to cooperate in the study. Each school was contacted twice. Eighty-three percent of the schools participated.

My original study sought to accomplish two objectives (Carpenter 1986). The first was to provide a baseline, descriptive analysis of the background, education, and employment history of these black female M.Div. students. In this regard, it was a corrective to the lack of such information in studies on women in the ministry. In particular, it was designed to some extent to compare the results with data received from the *Women of the Cloth* study published in 1983 by Carroll, Hargrove, and Lummis. This first descriptive study of women in the parish ministry failed to treat black women as a subset. The second objective of the study was to explore the relationship between how well black women were being placed in church-related employment and their church-like and sect-like characteristics. This chapter will address only the first set of results. The methodology used to accomplish both these objectives was a questionnaire of eighty-four variables—six professionalization variables, thirty-four sect-type variables, and forty-four intervening variables.

Of the seventy-seven schools that participated, 60 percent reported no black female M.Div. graduates. Thirty-one reported a total of 305 black female M.Div. graduates between 1972 and 1984 for whom addresses were available. Of this number, 269 appeared to have received the two mailings. A number of the mailings were returned because of incorrect addresses. Some were received too late or were incomplete. In some cases, the respondent indicated that she did not complete an M.Div. degree, or she was not black, or he was not female. In one case, she finished prior to 1972. Of the 269 identifiable graduates, 120 returned a useable questionnaire. This was a return rate of 45 percent.

The women in the sample were graduated from thirty-five different seminaries and were members of twenty-three different denominations. Twenty-four of the graduates were granted their degrees from the Interdenominational Theological Center in Atlanta, which is made up of six different institutions. This school provided seventy-one names and addresses of black female M.Div. graduates. Second in graduates yielded was Howard University Divinity School with twenty-two names and addresses. Nine of them are represented in the sample. Pittsburgh Theological, Virginia Union University Theological Seminary, and Union Theological Seminary in New York have eight graduates each in the sample. Yale University Divinity School, Duke University Divinity School, and Garrett-Evangelical Theological Seminary are also relatively highly represented. The other twenty-seven institutions are represented by three or fewer graduates each.

Those women affiliated with white, mainline denominations were the majority of the respondents at 61 percent. The Baptists were 13 percent; the African Methodist Episcopal, African Methodist Episcopal Zion, and Christian Methodist Episcopal churches were 13 percent; the Pentecostals 9 percent; the non-Pentecostal fundamentalists 2 percent; and all others 2 percent. The Baptists (excluding the American Baptists) and historically Black Methodists are equally represented in this sample. The United Methodists, Presbyterians, and American Baptists account for the lion's share of those women who were in white, mainline denominations.

Cultural Lag

One of the sociological concepts most helpful in understanding the placement of black female M.Div. graduates as a social problem is the concept of cultural lag. The elements of society do not change at the same rate of speed or with the same intensity and completeness. In his classic statement, William F. Ogburn observed:

> The thesis is that the various parts of modern culture are not changing at the same rate...and since there is a correlation and interdependence of parts, a rapid change in one part of our culture requires readjustments through other changes in the various correlated parts of culture. (Ogburn, 200)

While structures of major institutions such as seminaries and churches change slowly, the values deeply imbedded in the personality change even more slowly, often imperceptibly. This situation gives rise to social problems indicative of the one addressed in this book. Values that have been incorporated into the personality become an integral part of it. Any change that threatens these values becomes a threat to the personality itself. This is especially true of the religious person who reacts emotionally to any attempt to deny the revealed truths of his or her faith. For many, the prohibition against women preaching or having authority over men is considered a revealed truth based upon biblical injunctions; therefore they resist it.

Frequently, changes in basic social institutions are viewed as subversive and destructive of underlying social values. Differences in this attitude contribute to the differential rate of change between the various elements. Further, the differential rate of social change reflects the deliberate action of vested interests in delaying certain innovations. A vested interest is an individual, group, or institution with a preferred position in things as they are. These persons or groups resist changes that threaten their position. As pointed out by H. G. Barnett:

> The reception given to a new idea is not so fortuitous and unpredictable as it sometimes appears to be...There are certain situational features connected with it which pre-dispose those to whom it is introduced either to accept or reject it. (Barnett, 313)

Among these "situational features" are the basic values of the society. The concept of cultural lag is an important one for understanding the problem at hand. It focuses on the dialectical relationship between innovative ideas, such as the full equality of women and professional education, and conservative ideas, such as utilizing one or two biblical proof texts to circumscribe the role of women in the church and the notion of a hierarchical chain of command—male over female. These values have imbedded themselves in institutional structures, specifically, seminaries and churches. Seminaries in the midst of very recent changes have embraced a more egalitarian view of the status and role of women in the church at a more rapid rate than most churches, which tend to be more conservative.

Professionalization of the Ministry

The professionalization of the ministry can be understood sociologically as an outgrowth of the historical development of religious movements in America and the modernization of American society. According to Peter Berger, modernization is a process based on technological production and/or bureaucracy, characterized by rationality, specialization, large scale organization, the compartmentalization of various facets of the lives of the individuals, and a moralized anonymity that respects functions rather than persons (Berger et al.). The sociologist Max Weber has defined three types of authority exercised by leaders: (1) Traditional authority rests "on an established belief in the sanctity of immemorial traditions and the legitimacy of those exercising authority over them." (2) Charismatic authority rests "on devotion to the exceptional sanctity, heroism, or exemplary character of an individual person." (3) Rational-legal authority rests "on a belief in the legality of enacted rules and the right of those elevated to authority under such rules to issue commands" (Weber, 212). The last, rational-legal, is consistent with the term *professionalization*. It is based upon educational programs usually at the graduate level. High status is granted when one's specialty is subject only to peer review. Historically, the clergy in America was one of the first occupational groups to be professionalized.

Ordination

It was necessary to place in operation a definition of professionalization so it could be quantified for further analysis. The first variable delineated was ordination or certification.

Given the modernization of American Protestantism, ordination to the "set apart" ministry, usually with the laying on of hands by church leaders, and the granting of all the rights and privileges afforded the clergy is the primary basis upon which professionalization rests. Although the criteria for various religious groups may differ, there is a well-articulated way in which candidates for the ministry satisfy the requirements for such ordination. Over and above a graduate degree, and sometimes without it, the individual must have some recognized church body sanction or certify that he or she is fit for Christian ministry. For women, the key consideration is whether or not they can be fully ordained to the same high offices as the male clergy.

Employment

The second variable delineated in the study was "Full-time Salaried Employment in a Church-related Occupation." Since professionalization rests upon functional definitions, it is important that women ministers be employed by the institutions they serve. Again, the modernization of work has imposed a standard whereby the worth of a function is measured by the price it can command. While ministers are among the lowest-paid professionals, there must be some remuneration for their services, if they are to be viewed as peers in the professional matrix. Although part-time employment is sometimes desirable, the full test of being professional is full-time work. For purposes of measuring this variable, full-time church-related employment was considered high professionalization. The focus of this study is the ministry as a profession. While it is commendable that women with seminary degrees engage in creative and helpful secular work, often because it is the only avenue open to them, the task at hand is to keep the study within the exploration of ministerial professionalization. It does not mean that a person is not a professional if she does not meet this criterion; it means that she is not a professional minister. The development of a professional ministerial self is crucially important to the woman minister.

Church-related employment was defined as any of the ministerial type jobs for which the M.Div. degree traditionally prepares persons and which most frequently requires some religious body to certify that the applicant or candidate is ordained. This definition incorporates a wide variety of ministries, unlike *Women of the Cloth,* which restricted its definition of women clergy to those salaried in parish settings only. In that study, the terms minister and pastor were used simultaneously (Carroll, Hargrove and Lummis, 7). Table 4 lists some of the job categories that were considered church-related.

To quantify professionalization, each woman's employment history following graduation from seminary was reviewed and was coded based upon the *percent of time* spent in full-time church-related employment, part-time church-related employment, full-time nonchurch-related employment, part-time nonchurch-related employment, and unemployment. Intervals of 25 percent of the time were utilized.

Forty-four percent of these women worked 100 percent of the time since finishing seminary in full-time church-related employment. An additional 7 percent worked at least three-fourths of the time in full-time church-related employment. Relatively small percentages of these women are working in nonchurch-related employment on a permanent basis. Looking only at 1984, 65 percent were working in full-time church-related employment.

TABLE 4
Types of Church-related Employment

Associate Pastors	Students, teaching assistants in theological education
Christian education specialists— directors, publishers, writers, and editors of religious literature	Chaplains military, hospital, and prison
Campus ministers	Pastoral counselors clinical settings, congregational settings, and private practice
Christian school teachers and administrators— private parochial education	Ministers of Music
Denominationally and ecumenically affiliated agency staff	Pastors
Denominational office executives and associates at both regional and national levels	Administrators of agencies and organizations that relate to religiously-oriented philanthropy, publication, accreditation, mission, and interpretation
Higher education— seminary professors and college professors of religion, deans of schools of higher education	Missionaries
	Young Women's Christian Association and Young Men's Christian Association Staff

Six percent of the graduates have been 100 percent unemployed. One of the findings of the study is that age is correlated with unemployment. This can be explained in part by the fact that some retired women pursue the M.Div. degree, though they have no intention of, or are inhibited from, working in another professional position. They give enormous leadership on a volunteer or honorarium basis. Seventy-four percent have been unemployed less than one-fourth of the time, most of them not at all. These data reveal that this is a highly professionalized group. Jones and Taylor reported that only one-third of their sample of clergywomen was able to move directly into ministerial positions upon completion of education and certification (Jones and Taylor 1965). The present findings are more encouraging.

Table 5 gives the cumulative numbers and percentages of employers. The 120 graduates in the sample reported 213 different employers.

TABLE 5
Cumulative Numbers and Percentages of Employers

	Numbers	Percentages
Local Church	71	33
Educational Institutions	47	22
Denomination	15	7
Government, Military, Social Services	32	15
Health Organization	24	11
Counseling Organization	2	1
Ecumenical Organization	10	5
Other	12	6
	213	

TABLE 6
Cumulative Numbers and Percentages of Job Titles

	Numbers	Percentages
Pastor	26	12
Associate Pastor	43	20
Teacher, Director of Religious Education, Professor	39	18
Counselor	11	5
Social Service Professional	13	6
Chaplain or Campus Minister	45	21
Consultant	7	3
Denominational Executive/Staff	7	3
Other	23	11
	214	

Table 6 gives the cumulative numbers and percentages of job titles, 214 of which are reported by the sample of 120 graduates.

Denominational staff or executive did not surface as significant career paths for black women. This may be explained by two factors. First, 60 percent of these women are members of predominantly white denominations. Traditionally, denominational staffs only have opportunities for limited numbers of ethnic minorities to serve at regional and national levels. Second, most of the historically black denominations employ fewer administrative-type clergy. These denominations have very loosely structured offices at the national level. It is clear that for blacks, the most numerous positions are at the local church level, in military, hospital, and prison chaplaincies, and in the educational arena. The number of associate positions held by these women is surprising. The current findings reveal that the women in the survey have held forty-three different jobs as associate or supply ministers. Only a few of these positions were in white congregations. The total number of jobs in which women served as pastors was twenty-six, roughly 12 percent of the sample. Most of these women were in their first pastorate.

Table 7 gives the cumulative numbers and percentages of sizes of churches that employ these women. The sample of 120 graduates reported seventy-four churches in which they have worked either as pastors or associate pastors.

TABLE 7
Cumulative Numbers and Percentages of Church Sizes

Size	Numbers	Percentages
1–99	19	26
100–199	22	30
200–299	12	16
300–399	3	4
400–499	-	-
500–599	6	8
600–699	5	7
700 or more	7	9
	74	

Church size indicates a higher percentage of churches with fewer than 100 members than reported in the *Women of the Cloth* study (26 to 18 percent). These clergywomen worked in larger churches, generally. For example, 20 percent of the women studied worked in churches with 700 or more members, while only 9 percent of the present study did the same. Seventy-two percent of the black women in the present study work in churches with under 300 members.

These data substantiate other studies that show that women are assigned or called to smaller churches. Of course, part of the reason for this is their relative inexperience in ministry. Fifty percent of them finished seminary in the past three years. Only time will reveal whether there are opportunities for this type of career mobility.

Table 8 gives the cumulative numbers and percentages of salaries. The sample of 120 graduates reports 190 positions for which salaries are given.

TABLE 8
Cumulative Numbers and Percentages of Salaries

Size	Numbers	Percentages
Under $5,000	49	26
$5,000–$9,999	27	1
$10,000–$14,999	46	24
$15,000–$19,999	25	13
$20,000–$24,999	20	11
$25,000–$29,999	10	5
$30,000 and over	13	7
	190	

These data reveal the low salaries received by women ministers. Included in these figures and somewhat deflating them are part-time jobs. On the other hand, also included and somewhat inflating these figures are nonchurch-related jobs. The highest church-related salaries were paid to institutional chaplains–military, prison, and hospital. Educational institutions paid moderately well.

The cost of professionalization for black women clergy is an important issue, especially for the woman who is already established in another higher-paying career. When she enters the professional model of ministry, she must start at the entry level all over again; some are willing to go through this experience. It is becoming less and less of a problem for younger women who are able to move into such positions directly from seminary.

The sample of 120 graduates reports 212 positions in seven regions of the United States. The Mideast provides the largest number of jobs: 35 percent. The Southeast is close behind with 31 percent, followed by the Great Lakes region with 12 percent. The remaining 19 percent are spread in other regions of the United States, and 3 percent are outside the United States.

Career Goals

Table 9 reflects the career goals of the sample. Upon entering seminary, three goals had almost equal claim on the career aspirations of the respondents. These were specialized ministries, such as counseling and chaplaincy, 24 percent; parish ministry, such as pastor and associate pastor, 23 percent; and the teaching ministry, such as Christian education and college/seminary teaching, 20 percent. Only

TABLE 9
Percentages of Career Goals

Career Goals	Entering Seminary	Completing Seminary	Currently Enrolled
Specialized Ministries	24.4	17.6	21.4
Parish	22.7	44.5	38.5
Educational Ministry	20.2	17.6	18.8
Social Change Ministry	2.5	0.8	2.6
Executive Ministry	3.4	4.2	5.1
Unsure	10.9	5.0	5.1
Higher Education per se	10.1	5.0	3.4
Ordination	5.0	4.2	3.4
No. of Responses	119	119	117

11 percent entered seminary unsure of their goals. Another 5 percent entered seeking ordination

A major shift occurs as a result of the seminary experience. The percentage of these women who focused on a parish career almost doubled—from 23 to 45 percent. There is a corresponding decline in specialized ministries as a goal—from 24 to 18 percent. This may be related to the fact that most specialized ministries prefer persons who have had prior pastoral experience. It may also reflect what *Women of the Cloth* documented: "Women who come to seminary are often reluctant to articulate their pastoral aspirations for fear of lower acceptance" (Carroll, Hargrove, and Lummis, 231–32). Less of a decline occurs in the teaching area. Moving from 20 to 18 percent, the appeal of educational ministries holds more firmly.

Again the pattern of career goals shifts when one examines the goals indicated after some experience in the ministry. Parish ministry still holds the lead at 39 percent, but this represents a substantial drop. The largest increase is in specialized ministries, which rises to 21 percent—not quite as high as when these women entered seminary—gaining three percentage points. One reason specialized ministry may gain is that it normally pays higher salaries, since institutional settings that employ ministers can usually afford to pay more than churches. The teaching ministry remains nearly the same throughout, gaining slightly with ministerial experience. An area of increase with experience is social change or community outreach ministry. After seminary, this is a goal for less than 10 percent of the graduates. With experience after seminary, this area of service appeals to almost 26 percent of the women, at almost the same level as when they entered seminary. What may be happening is that women are learning to transfer skills and interests acquired prior to seminary. Just as education is a popular career before seminary, social work and community organization also rank high as previous careers.

Reviewing the shifting patterns of career aspirations, it is significant that the M.Div. seminary experience seems to draw these women toward the parish ministry. This is probably due to the fact that the curriculum is biased in this direction, and it is also due to their encounters with female-pastor role models in the seminary's faculty and student body. Its pull is lessened after some years in the ministry. In addition to the attractiveness of a higher salary, this phenomenon may be induced by the reality of parish life or difficulties perceived as unique to women. The explanation for this must be left to future research.

Factors That Promote and Inhibit Professionalization

Our final consideration will be the factors perceived as promoting or inhibiting professionalization. These women could give three different answers. Fifteen percent indicate education as the most powerful factor in promoting professionalization. In most cases, the women are referring to the positive effects of attaining a theological education. In a few cases, a certain type of education, namely denominationally sponsored seminaries, are viewed as more advantageous to career enhancement.

Apparently, education is perceived as an important legitimizing and enabling element in professionalization. This is an excellent example of how education can provide access to new opportunities for nontraditional groups or persons who have been discriminated against. For this reason, educational attainment has been one of the central strategies for black improvement within the American economy and job market. It seems that these women regard their investment in education as highly valuable. This coincides with the findings in the *Women of the Cloth* study (Carroll, Hargrove, and Lummis, 83).

Forty percent of the women indicate personal qualities as the most powerful factor that promotes professionalization for black female clergy. The helpful qualities include being realistic, being good at public relations, being political, having confidence, and exercising discipline. Others indicate that prior experience with laity and clergy, assertiveness, and a willingness to work much harder than men are helpful. Twenty-five percent state that structural factors are the most powerful. Structural factors include more viable salaries for women, affirmative action goals, networking with other women, and assigning women to larger churches. The women also cite the positive influence of seeing more black female clergy as role models and in key leadership positions. Some women feel denominational systems that are connectional and guarantee placement after ordination enhance women's advancement.

These women stated that sexism is the single strongest factor that inhibits the professionalization of black clergywomen. Sexism was articulated as the idea that women are not as capable as men, that women will lead to the ghettoization of the ordained ministry, sex role stereotyping that limits women to being evangelists and missionaries, and the idea that if a woman marries a minister she can have the best of both worlds.

Clergy and structural factors tied at 19 percent for the next most powerful influence against professionalization. Here the male clergy are accused of being insecure, less educated, and afraid of excellence and competition from the women. While criticism of the clergy does not surface as an inhibiting factor to ordination, the male-dominated clergy is perceived as an inhibitor to women's securing salaried, full-time church-related employment. Women sense a lack of peer support and isolation.

Further structural factors cited as inhibitors include antifeminine biblical/theological and doctrinal interpretations, conservative views, and the misconception of ministry as patriarchal, fear of change, unequal salaries, and the scarcity of administrative positions. The numerical scarcity of black women clergy and their placement at low membership churches was also cited. Some of the women feel that they have few advocates on regional and national levels.

It is interesting to compare dimensions helpful and inhibiting to ordination and professionalization. Table 10 reflects such a composite.

Personal qualities and education are perceived as the major factors in promoting and helping to attain professionalization and ordination. Structural factors are perceived as stronger obstacles and inhibitors to ordination and professionalization. While the support of family and friends ranks highly as a motivator toward ordination, its influence is slight in all other categories. Sexism is a major negative influence that makes both goals hard to attain. The lack of support of other clergy, the majority of whom are male, surfaces as a

TABLE 10
Cumulative Percentages for Factors That Promote and Inhibit Professionalization and Ordination

	Promotes Professional- ization	Helpful toward Ordination	Inhibits Professional- ization	Obstacles to Ordination
Structural	23	18	26	26
Personal	34	25	12	15
Education	20	22	5	6
Clergy	10	16	15	9
Family, Friends	5	15	4	8
Sexism			23	16
Other	8	3	15	20

significant inhibitor. This would lead one to conclude that if we want to advance professionalization among black female M.Div. graduates, strategies must be developed that address structural barriers, sexism, and ways to acquire the support of male clergy.

Male Referent for God

Only 35 percent of these women used any kind of male referent in their brief, written statements about God. Apparently the seminaries' shift to the use of inclusive language has been internalized well by these respondents. The most popular descriptor given God was Creator. Fifty-one percent used this in their first response. Coming in a distant second and third were words or phrases delineating attributes that described God (16 percent) and delineating the essence or being of God (15 percent).

Summary

Black women attended university-related seminaries in disproportionately higher numbers than their denominational counterparts (13 percent in *Women of the Cloth* to 24 percent in the present study; cf. Carroll, Hargrove, and Lummis, 79). More than half of them transferred into their present denomination from another denomination; 61 percent were affiliated with predominantly white, mainline denominations. Of those who transferred to other denominations, one-third did so because of perceived greater opportunity for ordination and employment; 51 percent of them were single; half of them came into the ministry from another career, and those who were in other professions previously seemed to pursue church-related employment more assiduously. Fifty percent were affiliated with denominations that did not ordain women until 1950 or later; half finished seminary after 1982. Seminary education rated highly as a most helpful factor in achieving ordination. Ordination was not a problem for most of these women. The socialization that occurs in seminary appears to have led a number of women to change their career aspirations away from specialized forms of ministry and toward parish ministry. Sixty-five percent of the sample were working in full-time church-related employment in 1984. This demonstrates some improvement in professionalization. Only 44 percent of the jobs reported over the entire twelve-year period under study were in full-time church-related employment.

Those agencies that employed the largest number of these women were local churches, educational institutions, and government agencies, which include military and other types of chaplaincies. The titles most frequently held were chaplain or campus minister, associate pastor, and educator. Most of the graduates earned annually $15,000 or less. Thirty-seven percent worked part-time for a period after graduating from seminary. The majority worked in the Mideast and Southeast regions of the country. Most were addressed with the title "Reverend." They cited personal qualities, structural openness, and seminary education as the factors most important in promoting professionalization.

The findings of this study are applicable only to black, seminary-trained women. But this is the group of women ministers who are the primary concern of theological education. These findings have important implications for theological education in the areas of recruitment, advisement, curriculum, and advocacy. The phenomenon of black women in ministry is not new, but their entry into the professional model of ministry is a recent, positive, and persistent trend. Theological education is the most important gatekeeper of this arena.

Postscript

The good news is that these women are working, more and more of them in full-time church-related employment, for which their ordination degrees have prepared them. Here is something old and something new. Black women as ministers and preachers date back to the times of slavery. But a new dimension has emerged. Admittedly, educated middle-class blacks have historically left the black Baptist and Methodist churches for mainline, white denominations. But some black women are feeling put out because of sexism and discrimination. Many of them do not want to leave. They leave to engage in a professional model of ministry, in denominations that are relatively new to them. This is reminiscent of Hagar, who was thrown out of Abraham's house, but whose descendants, the children of Ishmael, still challenge the Middle East, Africa, and India. And there was Joseph, sold into slavery by his brothers, to later save his father's house; and then also Esther, who was called to the King's house, out from among her own people, for a special time of threatening and salvation; and finally, Jesus, rejected by his own, but to become the chief cornerstone of the Gentiles. Perhaps some have to leave in order to be the impetus for saving others. Judgment is upon the church wherever sexism can be identified. The black church is no exception. One would have expected that the black church, that great champion of liberation and full equality, would already know that none are free until all are free. When up to 80 percent of the membership is female, what metanoia will break the yoke of a minority oppressing a majority?

The New Jerusalem is still a powerful image, for its lyrics say that "all who would could enter in and none will be denied." The kingdom of God shall have arrived for black clergywomen when a child can answer a telephone call for "Reverend Carpenter" with, "Which one?" and no one is offended. There is no doubt but that the seeds of the kingdom are already with us.

Sarah

"I work, but it is not paid work," is the comment of Sarah, a black woman minister from California. She reported that her church has seventy members and is growing very slowly. Her greatest opportunities to use the knowledge and skills gained from her M.Div. degree are in the areas of teaching, worship, preaching, and committee responsibilities. However, her greatest challenges come from what she views as the disparity between the treatment of women clergy and that of male clergy. Her reception as a woman minister has "run the gamut from very closed and conservative to extremely open and accepting encounters." Sarah feels that there is an implicit problem for clergywomen in that the ministry is viewed as a male bastion, a protected profession where men are given greater respect. She admits to having experienced divisive undercurrents among male clergy that consist of sexual harassment, employment discrimination, and salary disparity. According to her, there is a world of difference between the plight of male and female M.Div. graduates. Sarah says, "The male is going to have the support of a spouse to help with parenting and more." This is often not so with the female graduate who must usually parent and tend to ministerial concerns simultaneously. She has also observed an erroneous but prevailing view in many churches that the male head of house needs more money than the female single parent.

I have experienced the preceding as true. While serving on the hiring committee for a male associate minister, I was surprised at the amenities that were offered to my male associate and the concern expressed for his family. Although I had two children in graduate school at the time, no such concern was ever expressed regarding the financial responsibilities of my family. This matter of the perception of need is a critical issue since crucial financial decisions are often in the hands of male leadership within the church. Male lay leaders seem to be more respectful of the financial needs of male clergy than those of female clergy.

Our reverend from California reported that before she assumed her present ministerial position, the previous male minister had the services of a full-time secretary. When she arrived, the position was downgraded to a part-time secretary, and later to no secretary. When she commented upon the need to replace the secretary, a church official asked, "Don't you type?"

When I asked if she was a member of a support group, Sarah indicated that she used to be part of a women ministers group, but she did not find it very helpful. She was viewed as an outsider because she was not in full-time ministry. She commented on the hierarchical nature of the group as a negative factor. Tragically, her mentor in the ministry died, and she stated, "I'm not looking for another." Sarah has mentored other women by sharing her experiences and directing them to resources. However, she does not mentor other women ministers with regard to their seeking positions within the church.

Ironically, this type of mentoring and assistance can often create stress for the few women pastors who have been successful in maintaining paid positions. When other women ministers come looking for their help, there is often the expectation that, as women, they will be more sympathetic to the plight of other women. This phenomenon raises differing levels of difficulty. First of all, when a woman has just arrived and is viewed as experimental, most congregations become nervous when they see the female pastor elevating larger and larger numbers of women assistants. In addition, many women and men in the congregation believe that where there is a woman minister, there must be a man to balance the team. One unpaid woman on a ministerial staff commented to me that to see too many women in the pulpit seems "unnatural." This mentality places pressure upon women pastors to look for male assistants. However, after fifteen years of employing only male associates, I am now trying to provide a paid opportunity for a woman assistant to the pastor in my own congregation despite the pressure to add a male assistant for "balance." The shame of this situation is that when there were only male ministers in the pulpit, very little discomfort was voiced by most of the parishioners in the congregations. Thus, this is further evidence of the slow degree of social change exhibited within a conservative institution such as the church.

Returning to Sarah, she modifies her normal dress very little when she is in the pulpit. Her only concession is that she does not wear dangling earrings, since she has noticed that they can be distracting. Otherwise, her clergy dress ranges from jeans to long skirts to traditional clergy robes. She relished the memory that right before our interview she had preached in a pink shirt and pink jeans.

Sarah's community involvement is primarily through her congregation that sponsors ministries in the areas of peace witness, war tax resistance, and a food pantry. Her leisure time is spent studying and dancing. Her devotional life consists of meditation, prayer, rest, and relaxation. She is currently in Ph.D. studies in the history of religions. If she were to take continuing education courses for greater competency in ministry, she said they would be in the area of economic justice issues for women. In addition to the M.Div. degree, Sarah has earned another master's degree in counseling. She is "learning not to be defined by what I do, but by who I am— what kind of person I am." She believes that her most effective gifts for ministry are "teaching, preaching, and organizing."

When asked what needs to be done to improve the situation of black clergywomen, she pointed out a need for black women clergy to build their own levels of economic support. Women establishing churches of their own was one way she felt that this could be accomplished. She thought that women ministers would continue to be viewed competitively until more and more of them are visibly placed in paid positions, both parish and nonparish.

When asked what sources of power she possessed, this woman could not cite any. She preferred the term *strength*. Her source of strength is her belief in God, who is good and caring. Her favorite and most used image of God is as the earth and trees. Her favorite and most used image of Christ is as human and forgiving. What she emphasizes most about Christ is his ability to seek the good in all situations.

The above-mentioned profile casts light on the situation of many contemporary African American clergywomen. They are highly educated and freely give of their ministerial services, often without compensation. They are keenly aware of the double standards and sexism in the church and society. While they are accepted in some places, they know that they are not accepted everywhere. This lack of acceptance can range from not being acknowledged as legitimate to being assigned to restrictive, usually nonpaid, roles within the church. Unpredictable negative encounters in the church are like land mines that explode in the face, leaving casualties. In some cases, limbs of self-esteem, confidence, and trust are lost and replaced with edges of suspicion, which some men and women in the church call bitterness. These women know that there are casualties in this profession, and sometimes they imagine that they may become one of them.

4

An Emerging Portrait of Black Female Master of Divinity Clergy

At all places of encounter in the laity—the local congregation, the local community, the larger church (denomination), society in general, and even among female colleagues in the ministry—expressions of rejection directed toward black female Master of Divinity (M.Div.) clergy were frequent and disparaging. The following descriptive statements exemplify the nature of negative reactions from the congregational level.

The first black female ordained in New England in her denomination reported in a telephone interview that at the first church she was assigned to, 50 percent of the members were for her and 50 percent were against her. At the second church, 25 percent were for her and 75 percent were against her. At the third church, 10 percent were for her and 90 percent were against her. This traumatic set of experiences led her to ask for a leave of absence. Fortunately, she has returned to a situation where 90 percent are for her and 10 percent are against her. She felt much better in the final situation. Some women have left the ministry for this reason. One woman said, "It's not what I thought it would be."

One parishioner who belongs to a church pastored by a black woman said, "I don't invite my neighbor anymore. She's against women pastors. No matter how positive I am in my approach, she refuses to visit with us, though she is an active church woman."

After Women's Day, one of the youth ministry leaders said, "Pastor, I have to speak with you about the scriptures on women pastors. When I ask people to come to our church and tell them that my pastor is a woman, they drop their heads and decline. They are enthusiastic up to that point. I'm a new Christian and don't know the Bible well enough to be able to answer their complaints. It has happened so many times that I feel an urgent need to discuss it with you."

No matter how well-accomplished (with ordination and pastoral office), African American clergywomen are constantly made aware of rejection from the larger church and society. The following examples serve to illustrate this point. A black woman minister can admire a male minister for years before discovering that he resents her presence in the ministry. Such ministers are gracious when one is in their presence and very careful not to offend. One prominent minister speaking on men's ministry was asked how women pastors might play a role in men's ministry. He responded, "A woman minister can't do anything for me." Another who had worked with a woman associate for nine years said women ministers "carry too much feminist baggage." He has lowered his opinion of black women ministers in his locale and denomination. Often black women are told that they are bitter with complaint and therefore no one wants to associate with their cause. Such negativity leads to awkwardness at critical points in the performance of essential ministerial duties.

For instance, funerals and weddings can be very sticky times when the families involved belong to churches that do not affirm women pastors. Sometimes black women ministers must speak from platforms other than the pulpit from which black clergymen speak. Sometimes family and friends will not attend because a woman is presiding. Sometimes women ministers are escorted to sit with the pastor's wife and mother. She can enter a place with her male colleagues and then be separated from them because of restrictions that apply only to women. Such is the plight of women.

She stoically accepts negative behavior directed at her, but it still stings and burns. This isolates her. It feeds into her psyche the loneliness that all human beings seek to overcome. She wants to correct false beliefs but has to be silent, knowing that change in belief and attitude can only come when prejudice is challenged through direct experience in which she can minister at a deeper level in a person's life. The truth of her own reality is like fire shut up in her bones. Black clergywomen need to be acknowledged and affirmed as equals in the profession.

At times the ministry can be a profession without honor for black clergywomen. What honor is there when parishioners are told that, according to the Bible, they should not belong to a church pastored by a woman? What honor can there be when your husband is told that he should not come under the leadership of a woman? What honor is there when someone walks in off the street because he notices a female pastor's name on the church sign and then goes on to tell those within his hearing, "You should not have a woman pastor. This is what is wrong with the world today"? What honor is there when neighbors and friends of members consistently refuse to accept invitations to visit your church, or when Bible studies on the job plant doubt in the minds of members? What honor is there when male colleagues call your community leadership a liability to the movement? What honor is there when male clergy ask, "Whom do you have behind you and by what authority do you speak on behalf of the religious community to politicians, organizations, and media?" What honor is there when drivers who only have your name as "Reverend so and so" leave the airport and go back to the office, only to be sent back to look for a woman who is still waiting or by now has taken a taxi? Despite negative acts that erode her self-confidence and disempower her, African American clergywomen keep on going. In fact, they transcend the negative messages of their environment and lift their sights to higher sources of authority and power.

The Study

The purpose of my research is to assist black female M.Div. clergy, their families, their colleagues, future female graduates, seminaries, and churches in setting realistic goals for black female aspirants in ministry. To this end, my study is designed to elicit perceptions, attitudes, and reactions with respect to the interplay of problems and ministerial outcomes. This effort is critically important to the enterprise of many souls who press toward the mark of the high calling in Christ Jesus.

Methods used to collect data include: a fifteen-page questionnaire and a sixteen-page questionnaire mailed in 1985 and 1992, respectively, to female Master of Divinity graduates. The first data was collected as part of my doctoral dissertation (Carpenter 1986). The second study was an update of the first and included five additional graduating classes (1985–1989). Although they were seven years apart, the two surveys sought to measure similar information about black female M.Div. graduates over time. Further data from 1999 was also gathered.

The Association of Theological Schools, seminaries in the United States and Canada that recorded black female M.Div. graduates between 1972 and 1989, were contacted. Names and addresses were given to the researcher by each institution, and each woman was sent a sixteen-page questionnaire. In 1992, women from five more graduating classes were added (1985–1989).One hundred and twenty women, of the 309 contacted, responded in 1985 (39 percent), 203 of 605 responded in 1992 (34 percent).

The findings reported were derived from surveys conducted in 1985 and 1992. The participants earned a degree in a graduate theological school that was accredited by the Association of Theological Schools. Each woman received her M.Div., referred to as the ordination degree. Most of these women finished school with the idea of ordination and the hope of full-time ministry at some point in the future.

A telephone interview component served as a follow-up to the paper questionnaire. One of the telephone interview questions was, What do you perceive as sources of power in your ministry? Women said, in the following order of frequency: (1) Jesus, (2) faith in God, (3) the Holy Spirit, (4) scripture, (5) meditation, (6) people in the congregation, and (7) family. Such answers as these square very well with the seventeen sources of power detected through an analysis of the results of the questionnaire. Seventeen sources of power were identified among black female M.Div. clergy in this study. Those sources are: (1) increasing number, (2) ordination, (3) seminary experience, (4) educational credential, that is, the M.Div. degree, (5) womanist and liberationist theology, (6) spirituality, (7) mentors, (8) role models, (9) supportive family, (10) personal attributes, (11) switching denominations, (12) position, (13) increasing salaries, (14) career goals, (15) age, (16) experience, and (17) people in the congregations they serve.

The largest percentage of the women was in The United Methodist Church (22 percent). The Black Baptists and Black Methodists accounted for the next two largest groups (13 percent each), and the Presbyterians were very close behind (11 percent). The American Baptists accounted for 10 percent, and another 17 percent were in other white mainline denominations. These six categories accounted for 76 percent of the black female M.Div. clergy. In 1992, half had switched their denomination of origin; one-fourth did so before seminary and another fourth did so during and after seminary.

When asked to identify their theological orientation, among those who only checked one answer, 13 percent checked womanist, 12 percent liberationist, 11 percent liberal, 10 percent traditional, and 9 percent evangelical. Twenty percent chose a womanist/liberationist combination. When all combinations were counted, womanist led all other designations at 29 percent, with liberationist at 28 percent and liberal at 23 percent.

These women lived in thirty states and as far away as Kenya, East Africa. They are well represented in Chicago and other parts of Illinois, in Maryland around the Baltimore-Washington corridor, in New York and New Jersey, in Massachusetts, Virginia, Georgia, and North Carolina. They were also found in Texas, Ohio, and Pennsylvania, especially in Philadelphia. In summary, they were located mainly on the East Coast and in Illinois, Ohio, and Texas.

These women were serving churches in paid and nonpaid positions of leadership. On the nonpaid side, these women had served in a wide variety of capacities. The three most common were: (1) guest speakers and preachers (56 percent), (2) members of regional boards and committees for the denomination (42 percent), and (3) counselors (37 percent).

Seven other positions ranked sufficiently high for this report. They are consultant (24 percent), professor (19 percent), hospital chaplain (19 percent), church administrator (13 percent), campus minister (13 percent), director of Christian education (13 percent), and youth minister (11 percent). The vast majority of these women have worked in these ten areas of ministry; speaking/preaching was first on the list at 55 percent and next came pastor at 48 percent (36 percent had pastored full time). When one combines campus ministry and military, prison, and hospital chaplaincy, institutional ministries account for 46 percent of all paid positions. Most of those not in church-related positions were schoolteachers (20 percent), counselors (16 percent), college professors (13 percent), and self-employed (14 percent). Teaching and counseling in nonchurch contexts may or may not be related to ministry.

Hagar

This woman's case is very helpful not only because she is one of those who have switched denominations from a historically black one to a white, mainline denomination, but because she represents the priestly, prophetic, and evangelistic strand within the black church. Hagar is a United Methodist woman from Kansas City who grew up in the National Baptist denomination. She was ordained deacon in 1985 and elder in 1987. Her husband is also a full-time minister who does not pastor a church, but is a conference officer. She is not able to be appointed in the same town as her husband. She believes that the conference does not give both members of black clergy couples equal appointments. "They want you to come cheap." She considers her husband to be very supportive of her ministry, and she cites this as one of her greatest strengths. "We tend to complement, rather than compete. We help each other in sermon preparation. At one point when my husband fell into a lake and broke his arm, I had to do his church and mine." They have two grown children, thirty-seven and forty-two years old.

This sixty-seven-year-old clergywoman does not have an appointment presently, but she blames this on the racial discrimination that exists within her denomination, not her gender. She does acknowledge, however, that women are always paid less for the same work. Before seminary she was a civil servant accounting supervisor. She feels that for her, ministry is always full-time, even when designated part-time. When she had ministerial appointments, they were in the $20,000–$29,999 range. Hagar does not feel that her M.Div. degree has been fully utilized, stating, "We [black women] are sent to small churches where we cannot use the things taught in seminary. You stagnate." She feels that white men and women get better appointments, while both black male and female clergy are stagnating in the region where she lives.

Hagar was a pioneer by being the first black woman to pastor in an all-white congregation. The last church she pastored was an ethnically mixed congregation. Her ministry currently consists of being a counselor in a mental health program. She also works as a volunteer with numerous community programs that include an AIDS support group, a program for persons with Alzheimer's disease, a grief ministry, a homeless ministry, a jail ministry, and with "Army folk." She has also served on the national level as chair of her denomination's commission on racism. Locally, she is active in trying to bring all the community ministers together as president of a local Ministerial Alliance and has participated in the installation of another woman pastor. Although she feels accepted by the majority in her denomination as a "pioneer" and has demonstrated her skills as an administrator, preacher, and youth minister, she admits, "Some stone walls are still put in your way." Based on her own experience, Hagar cites as one of the big problems facing black clergywomen the bishop's decision to force black women into churches that do not want them. "African American males will always get small to medium churches, but males are preferred before females," she comments while repeating three times that her bishop did not support her.

Hagar tried support groups, but these did not work well for her. She gets her support from a black professional women's group. She has no mentor. It has been her experience that "once ordained to elder, we no longer have mentors." She has never mentored other women in ministry, though her husband has. Hagar says she is highly liturgical. She wears makeup, but no fingernail polish, no jewelry, and no long fingernails. In the pulpit, she wears an alb with stoles to match the liturgical colors of the church year. Sometimes she wears a black clergy robe with two academic stripes on the sleeves, and when representing the church in the community, she wears a clerical blouse with a suit.

"In most churches I have pastored, the men are at home. More women come to church and bring the children," Hagar comments. So she has tried to stress the need for more men in the church, not just to fill certain offices or to fix the building, but to help spread the message of the gospel. Nevertheless, in her churches, women have held most offices.

In addition to serving on the Commission on Religion, Hagar has served her denomination by sitting on the Commission on the Status of Women, the nominating committee, and the Board of the Diaconal Ministry, and was an organizer of a spiritual formation program. She has been vice chair of a local correctional facility advisory committee, a board member for a community service organization, and the only black on the NAACP's Economic Development Committee, and has worked with Little Theatre. She also organized a local group called Concerned Parents and Citizens, whose purpose is to help keep kids in school. It is easy to see why this woman has no leisure time, though she loves to fish and bowl. She also delights in devotional time to pray, retreat, and walk. She would like to one day pursue a Doctor of Ministry degree in Spiritual Formation.

Hagar cites as her greatest accomplishment in ministry the ability to bring people to Christ. She went to a church of thirty-five members, and it grew to one hundred members. She was especially effective in building youth and young adult ministries. She considers herself to be gifted in preaching, teaching, and administration. Regarding African American women in ministry, she states, "The world needs to hear the genuineness of our calling. We bring something special...We are much more nurturing. That's appreciated by everyone." Her source of power is her belief in God and her belief that God is the controlling power. She also draws strength from the fact that her husband and family always encourage her in ministry. She considers inclusive language to be very important, saying, "I am not a fanatic. I correct people in a nice way." Her favorite image of God is as a Spirit form that can be male or female. She likes to think of God as a "mother hen." She prays to God "the Father and Mother," but realizes that most older people cannot deal with such an attribution.

For her, God is primarily the Liberator, the Sustainer, the One who delivers. Her favorite image of Christ is the Suffering Servant, Jesus as the Lamb of God who takes away the world's sins. Ideologically, she stresses a grace theology—"in dying he saved us." She regards Christ as her Father, Brother, and now her Mother, now that her mother is dead. The latter is especially comforting in the wake of the loss of her mother.

There are special challenges that confront dual career marriages, and Hagar's ease highlights the fact that the same difficulties confront clergy couples. In the case of clergy couples, the issue of the church's not giving each member of the couple an equally challenging and well-paid position is particularly problematic and calls attention to two factors. The first is the exploitative nature of the church, and the second is the old concept that as long as the family unit is provided for, there is no need to pay the wife an equitable salary. Here the church is caught in the cultural lag of social change. Hagar has experienced this firsthand and sees the institutional church standing as a conservator of older values as it struggles to affirm the newer value of equal pay for equal work for women. While the church prides itself in being a family, using such slogans as "A Family Church Serving the Family of God," traditional crippling family values continue to dominate its language and programming, in spite of the fact that the majority of its parishioners are living in nontraditional family configurations. In contemporary society, there has definitely been a major shift away from a majority of couple families to more and more single-headed families. This holds true not only in society, but also in the church pew. However, since the male clergy still maintain a semblance of the older family patterns, the institution of the church has postponed the need to modify its practiced views. Fortunately, it appears from the data in this study that female clergy are more representative of the larger culture. Also, they do not have much to lose if they abandon what is sometimes a dishonest facade of healthy, traditional family contexts. Regularly, the black male minister has been notorious for having both a wife and an assortment of promiscuous relationships at the same time. The Alban Institute sponsored a conference on women ministers in which it expressed the hope that women ministers would be willing to discuss matters of sexuality and the dynamics of sexual politics within the church.

Our female clergywoman from Kansas City is a great community activist. One of the bittersweet benefits of women's receiving the M.Div. degree and not being able to fully utilize it in full-time employment is that they make excellent volunteers for leadership in both social service and social action arenas at the denominational, ecumenical, and community levels. Again, this takes one back to the older, traditional models of mainstream, nonprofit organizations that depended on upper-middle class, well-educated white housewives to provide leadership or to support their husband's leadership. The difference here is that black women of the past always had to work to support their families and were, for the most part, unavailable to participate in such arenas. The women in this study could potentially become part of such a cadre of nonpaid church leaders. But as Hagar indicates, women called to the ministry are not happy with this after they have invested more than $50,000 in a professional education and sacrificed long hours and years to complete their degrees.

While not certain of the future, most of the female seminarians that I have known at Howard University over the past eighteen years have hoped to attain full-time ministry-related employment when they finish their studies. I am amazed at the lengths to which some of these divinity students go, in one case taking out a second mortgage on her home to finance her M.Div. Like all higher education, graduate theological education is an economic investment, so it is crucial for women to examine the return that they are receiving on their investments. Comparative research needs to be done regarding the economic fates of those black ministers who receive the M.Div. degree and those who do not. Is there a perception that there is no economic advantage to receiving the M.Div. degree? Some of the most popular black preachers in America who head very large churches do not have graduate theological degrees. Many have M.B.A.'s, law degrees, and other credentials, but often no graduate theological certification. A serious investigation into just how much seminary experience is actually used in the congregation remains a question.

Other questions that should be posed include: (1) What is the best kind of training to ensure the success of black women in the ministry? (2) How much does society value the scholarly training and professional certification of its clergy? (3) Does the black church value this training less than the white church? (4) For black female clergy, is an M.Div. degree an asset or a waste of time? Based upon my research, I have concluded that seminary education is a prime ingredient for the success of black female clergy.

We would call Hagar a community mother in the historic tradition. Such persons often are labeled "troublemakers" for their prophetic voices, but they are just the ones who can be counted on to participate in advancing a cause that helps to correct problems within the community. This is a great model in the spirit of Mary McLeod Bethune, Nannie Helen Burroughs, and Mary Church Terrell. Based upon their dedication and vocation to serve others, all of these women might have been ministers themselves had that option been available to them. We remember them because they organized institutions that have preserved their names and histories.

Women like Bethune, Terrell, and Burroughs have accomplished a great deal and do raise another observation with regard to ordained women who revert to operating more comfortably within female lay groups. Some women ministers can accomplish more in lay contexts, where the matter of legitimacy is not questioned. Hagar, for example, having been rejected by ecclesiastical circles, turned her energy to professional lay organizations, taking great pride in attacking social problems. She is proud of her accomplishments in this arena. It is indeed a ministry for the needs of people. The church should be proud of such women because they demonstrate what new models of ministry may look like. To such women ministers Zikmund, Lummis, and Chang dedicated their book *Clergywomen: An Uphill Calling.* The citation reads, "This book is dedicated to clergywomen who envision new forms of ministry for tomorrow's church."

Considering alternative modes of ministry for black women, the placement of black women in all-white churches is an interesting recent phenomenon. The first church I pastored was such a church, though it included one black family and another that had adopted two black children. I served as interim minister for five months, whereupon the pastor, who was on sabbatical, resigned from the church, left his family, and went on to become the first openly gay pastor of a church within my denomination in California. I took the congregation through the grief of losing their pastor under these circumstances. When my contract ended, I stayed on an additional month and was asked to become a candidate for permanent pastor. I declined, but I was struck by the close bonding that was possible between a black pastor and white parishioners. The *Washington Post's* senior religious editor did a large article on my ministry at this church entitled "Black women, white pulpits." This phenomenon is increasing the challenges of the traditional relationship between race and religion in America, since the church itself has remained one of the most segregated institutions in America. This has occurred because the black church is one of the four remaining vestiges of African and African American cultural preservation left in this country along with black colleges, fraternities, and sororities. This is an important function that all ethnic groups in America have appreciated. For example, the neighborhood Catholic church has been dominated by whatever the majority ethnic group is at that time. One of the differences between the Catholic and Protestant presence in black communities is that white clergy have led large black Catholic congregations, but not Protestant ones. But the notion of black clergy leading large white congregations or multicultural congregations, which tend to be predominately white, always seems to be classified as something new when it happens. This phenomenon needs to be measured in some way in order to document this growing trend; otherwise the perception of these appointments remains experimental, as isolated exceptions to the rule but not the norm.

In her case study, Hagar raised the issue of female clergy appointed to churches that are not ready to accept a woman. This matter of "forcing a woman" on a congregation places the woman in a hostile environment and creates stress both for the woman and for the congregation. As detailed earlier in this book, this very situation led one black clergywoman to take a leave of absence from the ministry. She later returned to a more affirming church, and she was then happier with her ministry. This is another land mine that ecclesiastical officials and women themselves should try to avoid, for it can produce the type of damage and bitterness for which black clergywomen are severely criticized. I remember meeting with a group of black women ministers and one woman remarked that she did not want to be part of a "bunch of bitter, complaining women." This woman was much younger and more successful than those meeting, and she failed to acknowledge how the advocacy of these older women had made her career possible. It is important for us all to listen to the horror stories of others so that those who have been wounded may begin to receive greater healing in our midst. Part of the healing comes when women who have not had negative experiences express appreciation for the pioneering women who bear the battle scars. Such sisters should be treated as wounded soldiers of valor to be honored.

In the case of Hagar, an older woman who has confronted both racism and sexism, for example, she is one who bears numerous battle scars. She feels that her refusal of an appointment by her denomination has turned her bishop against her and has prevented her from gaining a position that she deserves. She is one of the wounded soldiers who is still on the battlefield. Much of the competition and lack of support that black clergywomen experience when trying to come together is embodied in the failure to recognize that there is not a fair playing field with all persons starting at the same point. Some situations are tougher than others, and all women have not had the same resources available to them. This fact should be kept in mind as clergywomen come together. Special attention must be given to the non-elites, those pioneering clergywomen whose names are not as well known or whose churches are not as large as some or who do not presently have significant positions in ministry.

Turning to the evangelistic strand that peeks through in Hagar's interview, she cites "bringing people to Christ" as her greatest accomplishment in ministry. Recently she rejoiced that she led a thirty-seven-year-old and his son to be baptized. At this point her good National Baptist roots are displayed as well as something very important about black women preachers. Many of them have not lost their evangelistic emphasis. Much has been written about nineteenth-century, black, singing, evangelist women. One of the finest treatments of such women is in a doctoral dissertation written by Gloria Davis Goode in 1990, entitled "Preachers of the Word and Singers of the Gospel: The Ministry of Women among Nineteenth Century African Americans." Dr. Goode uses spiritual autobiographies of fourteen nineteenth-century women, whom she describes as non-elites, eclectics outside denominational churches that served as credible spokespersons for black culture. She shows how their calls to preach came out of their experiences of salvation and sanctification that further led them to being effective evangelists for Christ. Goode discusses such well-known black women ministers as Jarena Lee, Julia Foote, Rebecca Jackson, Maria Stewart, Zilpha Elaw, and Amanda Berry Smith. She additionally analyzes less well known black women such as Slavewoman Elizabeth, Chloe Spear, Sidonie Smith, Nancy Prince, Rebecca Steward, Mrs. Edward Mix, Harriette A. Baker, Hannah Carson, and Rebecca Perot.

This same spirit of evangelism persists in black preaching women of today. Although the women in this study have attended seminary, many of them have not lost the fervent black prayer traditions and evangelistic zeal out of which their calls to ministry were birthed. The same can be said of black male clergy. It seems that the black church, which addresses the common struggle of slavery and the triumphs of throwing off oppression, is in a sense still ecumenical. There is a black church because black Christians have consistently rejected white Christianity as totally theirs, since it was white Christianity that in large measure enslaved them. Black Christians became transdenominational. This is best expressed through the common corpus of black sacred music that is embraced and revered by most black Christians, regardless of their denominational affiliation. Therefore, in the black church, there has not been that division between the mainline and the evangelical right-wing Christians that is popularly discussed today.

With regard to the classification of Spirit-centered denominations in the Zikmund treatment (Zikmund, Lummis, Chang, 12–15), though the black church typically divides over the issue of speaking in tongues as a requirement, it remains a spirit-filled institution within all denominations, as documented in Lincoln and Mamiya's treatment where they characterize the black church as "neo-Pentecostal." While the Board of the Congress of National Black Churches normally focuses upon the seven largest historically black denominations, there are many other hybrid and Pentecostal black churches as well. In addition, black congregations within white denominations often resemble their historically black counterparts in worship style, if not in polity. Therefore, despite its numerous manifestations, the black church has managed to keep its spirit-filled, evangelistic thrust within its mainline expressions. This may be why some predominately white denominations now find that their ethnic churches, and particularly the African American churches, are growing while overall membership in these denominations is declining.

Finally, Hagar's experience reveals the high christology that remains in black religion. Howard Thurman once said to my seminary class, "You cannot take Jesus from black people." Although trained theologically to distinguish God from Jesus, blacks tend to start praying to God and end up calling on Jesus. In this study, large numbers said that sometimes God is Jesus Christ. In Hagar's case, Jesus fills every relationship—Father, Brother, and Mother— for he is the Suffering Servant who understands all her problems and struggles. When her mother is gone, Jesus becomes her mother. This revelation comes at the cross, where black people see in the face of Christ the suffering they have endured. Black women ministers still see their struggles in his face too. In the garden of agony, black women see in Jesus their own anguish. In his triumph over the grave, they see their own potential to succeed. Thus, the lines between God and Jesus become blurred, and black women can become more monistic than modern Christian theologians. After all, it was Jesus who shed His blood for our sins. He saved us, bought us, and taught us. The joy that he gave us continues to spill over into our testimonies, prayers, and exhortations. If God is our Creator and Liberator, Jesus is our Savior and Best Friend. The Holy Spirit is the presence and power of both God and Christ, alive and working in our lives to make us like the Holiness of God, a Sanctifier.

5

How They Overcame Spiritually

In the previous chapter, a general profile of black female Master of Divinity (M.Div.) clergy emerged as a reflection of their progress in the ministry. As in other areas of human endeavor, they experienced positive elements that were propelling and negative elements that were discouraging. This chapter examines and interprets their perceived sources of power that prevail even when the negatives seem to outweigh the positives.

The Participants

A glance at these black clergywomen's predecessors in ministry sheds some light on ancestral inheritance and a sense of responsibility among the present generation to prevail. Three waves of pioneer black women ministers are recognized. The subjects of this study compose the third wave.

The first wave of black clergywomen was the preaching, praying, and singing evangelist women of the late nineteenth century. The second wave was the twentieth-century black female leaders who headed churches that were small, self-established, perhaps inherited through the ministry of a male relative, usually a husband or father. The third wave is going where black women ministers before them have not gone, that is, into positions of leadership in the center of the church. No longer ministering from the margins, they have stepped into the pastoral arena of the dominant institutional church. These contemporary black clergywomen are leading larger, historic churches that were founded by persons other than themselves or their family members. Parallel to all these groups are the active laywomen who served in church positions as missionaries, educators, social workers, counselors, church administrators, and staff. Black women form the majority and backbone of the church in that they are the strongest constituency of the church in every way—numerically, financially, and programmatically. This makes them an important ally of the pastor.

Perceived Sources of Power

Seventeen sources of power were identified by black female M.Div. graduates in this study. The following are some sources of power for women in ministry: increasing numbers, the choice to switch denominations, theological orientation, geographic accessibility to theological schools, positions in ministry, marital status, career goals, mentors and role models, the practice of ministry, and spirituality.

When applicable, portions of Alice Walker's definition of womanist are given as subtitles to emphasize the spirit of the contemporary woman exemplified by the women in this study.

Increasing Numbers

The first source of power for black clergywomen is their growing numbers. In 1985 the seminaries reported 309 black female M.Div. clergy. In only five more years this had grown to 605. Twenty-three percent of those who completed the survey in 1985 also filled one out in 1992. Unless otherwise noted, the findings reported here are from the 1992 study.

Of the respondents, 90 percent were ordained. That is a powerful finding because it means that the issue of opposition to ordination, which was very troubling within certain denominations, seems to have been overcome by 90 percent of these women. In the seven-year gap between the two surveys, the number of women who were ordained rose from 76 percent in 1985 to 90 percent in 1992. Some of the 10 percent who were not ordained in the 1992 survey did not wish to be.

Switching Denominations

These contemporary womanists are "traditionally universalist" (Walker). In the 1985 study, 51 percent of the women had switched from their denominations of origin during and after seminary. This is a major change. It can be partly explained by the large numbers of blacks who joined predominately white denominations, particularly The United Methodist Church. Usually this occurred in conjunction with the attainment of higher education and upward social mobility. While 43 percent grew up in historically black denominations, only 27 percent remain. That is a 16 percent loss to the black denominations–thirty-three women in the 1992 study. According to Dr. C. Eric Lincoln and Lawrence Mamiya's estimate in their book *The Black Church in the African American Experience,* only 15 percent of all black clergy are seminary graduates. Looking at this study the question to be raised is, Can historically black denominations afford to lose 16 percent of their theologically trained women ministers? Obviously, they feel that they can, but graduates such as these thirty-three women, with the help of the resources of the black church, could be leaders in the struggle to improve the plight of the black community relative to school drop-outs, substance abuse, homicide, incarceration, inadequate health care, unemployment, underemployment, and abandoned, derelict urban housing. Black female M.Div. clergy switching from historically black denominations to mainline, white ones might be called a "brain drain" and increasingly a "leadership drain." This can be said because most of these women entered seminary as established professional, community, and church leaders.

In the fifties, there was a tendency for more highly educated, more affluent blacks to make such shifts to higher-class denominations. However, since the "Black is Beautiful" cultural revolution in the late 1960s, education alone has not led to such shifts, as blacks remain more and more loyal to their own roots and to a more Afrocentric perspective, especially in their churches. This is because black churches remain great cultural preserves and centers of power for the black community. Denominational switching on the part of these women is probably less attributable to social mobility and more attributable to sexist practices within the black church.

The biggest losers in this denominational switching were the National Baptists and the Missionary Baptists. The biggest gainers were the United Methodists and the Presbyterians. This raises serious concerns regarding the future role of women in the largest black denomination–the Baptists. There are early signs of a few openings for women, but overall, the outlook is grim. In most geographic areas of the country, Black Baptists still teach and preach against the ordination of women. Yet some of the women are courageously staying in the Baptist tradition that birthed their call. This is most likely when a benevolent pastor has established a positive, nurturing relationship with such women. It is risky, however, for if that pastor dies or leaves, she is at the mercy of the new pastor, who may not have a positive attitude toward women ministers. Then all the ground she thought she had gained is lost. There are many cases of such displaced women ministers.

Another limitation that is true for women ministers in all denominations is that women who have demonstrated that they are gifted for ministry are relegated to pulpits with little or no chances for mobility to larger churches. This can be extremely frustrating and confining, especially if their congregations plateau, and they feel that their leadership cannot take the people any further. It has been my experience that more progressive congregations can like the idea of a woman pastor, and later become less enamored with the idea as dynamics not thought out beforehand begin to surface. On first report, it seems that switching denominations is a reasonable solution to the problem of not having a rewarding place in which to fulfill one's vocation. However, there are five concerns that may limit the mobility of women who leave their churches of origin to join other denominations. These can be powerful currents that diminish their career mobility.

The first factor is a lack in generational depth. It relates to the family-dynasty nature of many black churches. The church arena is highly competitive, and there are often other ministers who have been waiting in line before these women arrive. Many of those who are waiting in line have sponsorship, especially those who are connected through family ties. The second factor is the questionable acceptance quotient. Church old-timers wonder if these newcomers to the denomination will stick with them and the traditions that have given them comfort in the past. The third factor is higher socioeconomic class. Often the members of the churches these women are transferring into are of a higher social class than those of the churches they are leaving. This may lead to an incongruity between the woman minister and her congregants with reference to social justice ministries. The fourth factor is change in worship style. These women may be coming from more spirit-filled, charismatic churches. While this may be welcomed initially as good for church renewal, there can be problems relative to how much change in worship style a congregation is willing to make within a particular length of time. The fifth factor is the perception of abandoning one's own people. This can lead to isolation among colleagues, which makes it more difficult for these women to experience visibility and sponsorship. In *The Irresistible Urge to Preach,* one clergywoman relates that when she joined a black church within a white denomination (United Methodist), she was accused of "turning her back on black folks" by a prominent African Methodist Episcopal pastor in her city (Meyers, 354).

Theological Orientation

In response to the inquiry about their theological orientation, "womanist" led all other designations. It is most remarkable that so many women chose womanist. None of the women in 1985 wrote womanist as the response to a similar, open-ended question. The term itself was then in its infancy stage.

Its origins can to traced to Alice Walker's *In Search of Our Mothers' Gardens.* Walker affirmed the history and importance of the experience of black women. She turned the spotlight on the uniqueness and complexity of black women's lives as they continually struggle to maintain life and to make it better for themselves and their families (Walker).

A womanist, according to Alice Walker, is one who is "outrageous, courageous, and willful in behavior" (Walker, xi). Usually a black mother charged her female daughters with this kind of assertiveness. Invariably, the child was seeking to know more and in greater depth than what was considered good for her. Walker says that a "womanist is responsible, in charge, serious" (Walker, xi). However, a womanist is not a "separatist," but "one who is committed to the survival and wholeness of an entire people, male and female, regardless" (Walker, xii).

The womanist tradition is identified with such notables as Harriet Tubman, Sojourner Truth, Maria Stewart, Anna Jones Cooper, Mary McLeod Bethune, Rosa Parks, Fannie Lou Hamer, and countless other women who have molded and shaped the womanist consciousness that now pervades twenty-first-century North America. This consciousness has resulted in a social and political praxis that is characterized by struggle, survival, self-determination, and freedom for others and themselves.

A womanist ideal cannot be understood apart from its historic context. The impulse for liberation and autonomy has been a perennial struggle for black women from the forcible removal of female slaves from West Africa up to the present time. Responsibility, wholeness, and resistance illustrate a womanist tradition of struggle among black women in overcoming the brutality of slavery, the dehumanization of segregation, and the injustice of discrimination to forge a new world for succeeding generations.

With the emergence of the womanist concept in the African American community, more black women are unashamedly claiming their places in the development of black history, culture, and religion. They are affirming their abilities to struggle against a pyramid of oppression that consists of racism, sexism, and classism. They are doing this while maintaining their families, churches, communities, and themselves. Womanist religious dialogue is contextualized in the life experiences of black women who have utilized the faith tradition for ontological affirmation, salvific regeneration, and social transformation.

Dr. Jacquelyn Grant, professor of theology at the Interdenominational Theological Center in Atlanta, Georgia, emphasizes that black women are among the poorest and the most oppressed people of the United States. Therefore, womanist theology speaks a liberating message to the lives and struggles of black women. When black women affirm that God is on the side of the oppressed, they are saying that "God is in solidarity with the struggles of those on the underside of humanity; those whose lives are bent and broken from the many levels of assault perpetrated against them" (Grant, 124). The fabric of black women's lives has been woven with the threads of spirituality, human compassion, and suffering.

The term *womanist* first emerged in black women's theological writing in 1985 when Katie Cannon adapted Alice Walker's definition of womanist for theological interpretation in "The Emergence of Black Feminist Consciousness," which was published in *Feminist Interpretation of the Bible* (Cannon 1985; cf. Sanders 1994). In the spring of 1986, Jacquelyn Grant published "Womanist Theology: Black Women's Experience as a Source for Doing Theology, with Special Reference to Christology" in the *Journal of the Interdenominational Theological Center*. In March 1987 Delores Williams published her article "Womanist Theology: Black Women's Voices" in *Christianity and Crisis*. These earliest pieces offered sources and methods for doing womanist theology and ethics as a discipline focused on the experiences of black women. In 1988 Dean Lawrence Jones of Howard University School of Divinity provided the necessary funds to convene a symposium of womanist scholars at the school. The result of this meeting was a continuation of the discussion at the American Academy of Religion. In 1989 the womanist group held its first consultation, and it was officially recognized in 1990. Each year a variety of papers have been presented and panel discussions are held. In 1989 the *Journal of Feminist Studies in Religion* printed a roundtable discussion initiated by Dr. Cheryl J. Sanders on "Christian Ethics and Theology in Womanist Perspective." Dr. Kelly Brown Douglas taught a course on womanist theology at Howard University School of Divinity. In response to the intergenerational dialogue between a mother and daughter found in Walker's definition of womanism, Douglas says: "This dialogue suggests three essentials for womanist pedagogy: it must provide students with an opportunity to dialogue with black women's history, with ordinary black women, and with each other" (Douglas).

The fact that only 2 percent of the women in the 1992 study chose *feminist* exclusively and only 8 percent in combination with *womanist* is interesting. It documents, to a large extent, the rejection of the white woman's struggle, labeled as feminist, as their own. On one hand, it affirms the urgency of the imperative for a distinct, female imaging of God, while on the other hand, it demonstrates the determination of black women to hallow out a space for the voice of God to speak through their unique experience. With the creation of black liberationist theology and feminist theology, books were written according to black men's and white women's understandings of faith, in addition to white men's theologies. Yet none of them spoke directly to the concerns of African American women (Wortman). Until womanist theology, black women had little opportunity to hear or read about theology from a black woman's point of view.

The rapid identification with the term *womanist,* which was imported from secular black women's literature into theological circles, testifies to the richness of black female spirituality and the long tradition of black women preachers and evangelists. The acceptance came also because of the profundity of Sojourner Truth's "Ain't I a Woman," and black women's familiarity with the cultural audacity of being womanish. Not without its problems, womanist seems to have appeal and endurance. Because it encompasses the well-being of gender, race, and class, it may prove to be sufficiently particular and universal at the same time. If so, it will be a helpful construct for speaking about God in an increasingly diverse society.

Liberationist theology, which encompasses black theology, remains strong, as it was in the 1985 study. This probably means that these women have a passion for the uplifting of black people. If so, the denominations into which they have switched have gained additional social justice advocates. Liberal theology reflects the majority of graduate theological schools in America, particularly those associated with large universities.

Geographic Accessibility to Theological Schools

The women in the 1992 study lived in thirty states and as far away as Kenya, East Africa. However, the majority were located mainly on the East Coast and in Illinois, Ohio, and Texas. Accessibility to educational opportunity and credentialling is a source of power for this emerging new leadership group. The three historically accredited, predominately black theological schools, Howard University, Virginia Union University, and the Interdenominational Theological Center, are conveniently located on the East Coast, which explains the higher enrollment of women from the East Coast.

Positionality in Ministry

These contemporary womanists are "responsible, in charge, serious" (Walker). These women had served the church in a wide variety of capacities in both paid and nonpaid positions. The three most common nonpaid roles were as guest speakers and preachers and as members of regional boards and committees for the denominations and counselors. Positions such as these lead to visibility, networking, and good contacts for future placements in paid positions. The denominations are benefiting from a pool of well-trained volunteer leaders. The caution I would offer here is that the denominations often benefit from these women's leadership without adequately rewarding them with a parallel career track. Most serve at the local and regional levels, and only a few are promoted to the national boards and committees. National exposure is better because there are very few jobs at the regional level, especially in denominations where the percentage of black congregations in a given region is quite small. Serving on national boards is more advantageous to placement if one is able to move geographically. Consequently, while such nonpaid activity can be rewarding to men, it may not lead to the personal rewards that these women deserve.

The vast majority of these women have worked in ten areas of ministry with speaking/preaching first on the list at 55 percent and serving as pastor second at 48 percent. Thirty-six percent have pastored full-time. This is more than triple the 11 percent who pastored full-time in 1985. Associate pastors were next at 36 percent. Counseling came next at 25 percent. This a healthy increase over the 14 percent who were working in counseling in 1985. Because of barriers within the church, these women are turning outside the church to institutional ministries for employment. This demonstrates the creativity and versatility of these women. The problem with this, however, is that the opportunity structure for the employment of these graduates is far greater among local churches, especially in the position of pastor. There are many more churches than there are other institutions with positions for ministers. If the church only pays one person, it is the pastor. As the number of black female M.Div. clergy grows, it is hoped that they will be able to fill more and more church-based, paid positions. Some will say that there is much unpaid ministry to be done. This is true and commendable, but the black church needs to ensure that its resources are invested wisely. Whoever it depends on to provide paid leadership—to vision, to manage, and to evaluate its life together—should be trusted as competent, compassionate, and of good character. Increasingly, women are among the best candidates for the job.

The fact that these women are still having difficulty being placed after seminary was illuminated by some of the nonchurch jobs that they held. A few black female M.Div. clergy were working as secretaries and blue-collar workers. Some women who are seminary graduates have returned to their first-career occupations after investing three years in study and after receiving years of low wages in a rather uneven ministerial career. In 1992, 10 percent were earning $10,000 or less; 42 percent were earning $30,000 or more seven years later in 1999.

Marital Status

These contemporary womanists "sometimes love" (Walker). Thirty-six percent of the respondents were married. This has remained rather constant, only slightly increased over 1985, when 34 percent were married. Twenty percent were divorced, up from those that were divorced in 1985. In the *Women of the Cloth* study, 55 percent of the women ministers were married and only 10 percent were divorced (Carroll, Hargrove, Lummis).

The findings of this study reveal a relatively high singleness rate of 66 percent among black female M.Div. clergy. This is a very high proportion. However, this exactly matches the figure reported by

Dr. Jwanza Kunjufu, who reported in his book *The Power, Passion, and Pain of Black Love* that two-thirds of all black professionals are single (Kunjufu).

Who would marry a woman minister, and how do these women find the support and intimacy that all persons need and deserve? These are important questions on which more research is needed. Singleness can also be a problem for placement. In the past, most churches wanted a married minister. The need to reinforce strong family values is great, and congregations want to see these values exemplified in their minister's family. There is a great deal of potential discrimination in this area, even though the laws of the land prohibit it. Churches seem to be more open toward remarried persons because they seem more acceptable than single, never married, or divorced persons, though happily this is changing.

Career Goals

These contemporary womanists are "outrageous, audacious courageous" (Walker). These women aspire to perform in all categories of positions in ministry. This section only addresses those jobs that at least 5 percent of the women checked. This means that at least ten women checked the goals mentioned below.

The only area of ministry that has lost ground is that of Christian education. Upon entering seminary, 8 percent aspired to be Christian educators. In part, this is because Christian education was the area most open to women in the past; but after attending seminary and after graduation, this specialty is no longer a goal for significant numbers of black female M.Div. clergy. This is probably because there are few paid positions solely in Christian education in the African American church. Where they exist, the salaries are quite low. Christian education has been traditionally dominated by the laity, as seen in the Sunday school movement in America. Only now is the black church beginning to realize its need for paid, professional help in the areas of publishing suitable religious literature, youth work, leadership training, and the establishment of independent Christian schools. As this awareness grows, more black female M.Div. clergy will choose this area of work.

The biggest gain is in the pastoral ministry, with pastor and associate pastor rising from 6 percent to 10 percent. Counseling as a career goal went from 5 percent upon entering seminary to 8 percent in 1992. Hospital chaplaincy rose to 6 percent on completion of seminary, but declined to an insignificant level in 1992. This is probably because the budgets for hospital chaplains have been greatly reduced, because hospitals themselves have suffered major financial problems recently. Finally, professor, consultant, and denominational executive emerged as frequent career aspirations in 1992. For the most part, these career aspirations were developed after leaving seminary.

Professor led the group in terms of growth. This may be explained by the increased numbers of women now teaching in seminaries and the fact that some of the black female M.Div. clergy have performed very well academically, often surpassing their male counterparts in academic rank. To some extent, women seminarians have created the need for additional female professors. A good number of seminaries now have more women students than men. With this drastic change in student profile has come the demand for more female professors. Even second-career women are continuing in doctorate degrees, which may qualify them for professorial positions.

Mentors and Role Models

These contemporary womanists are "wanting to know more" (Walker). Eighty percent of the respondents have had mentors, primarily male. Although the majority of mentors have been male, the women expressed a great need for female role models similar to that related in *The Irresistible Urge to Preach* (Meyers). Those studies revealed that while the women were being mentored by male leaders, it was not until they had seen a woman preaching or presiding in the pulpit that they achieved greater comfort with their own ministries.

This is further borne out in this study by looking at the listing of those who had three or more mentors. Not everyone answered this question. More women listed one mentor than listed two or three. Among the mentors mentioned first, 55 percent were male and 24 percent female; among those mentioned second, 40 percent were male and 23 percent female; and among those listed third, 20 percent were male and 19 percent female. Here the gender gap is almost closed for those who had three mentors. This could be explained by the time factor, indicating that as time passes, women are more likely to have contact and meaningful relationships with other women ministers. The other is the numerical factor, namely, that as a clergywoman expands to more than one mentor, she will be drawn to reach out to a same-sex clergyperson.

Practice of Ministry

These contemporary womanists are "traditionally capable" (Walker). These women practice ministry most often through teaching, administration, preaching, counseling, and visitation. Fifty-seven percent said they preach always and 34 percent said occasionally. It is clear from the responses that they would like to preach more often, both because they listed it among the three ministerial practices that they enjoy most (67 percent), and because they value it as helping people the most (68 percent). When asked what three activities they enjoyed most, 100 percent circled social services, 71 percent teaching and 67 percent preaching. Forty-eight percent of the respondents occasionally engaged in community and social action ministries, but it is still difficult for women ministers to head community and social action initiatives. This is because they tend to be politically based. Male clergy are unlikely to participate in community coalitions led by female clergy. Women ministers are seen as controversial and unable to solicit the necessary support among the male clergy. As one prominent pastor and community leader said, "Let's not push the women's leadership. It can be a liability."

Spirituality: Images and Attributes of God

These contemporary womanists "love the Spirit" (Walker). When asked to check the image of God that they thought of "most of the time" and "much of the time," Creator and Spirit tied at 97 percent, Wisdom was at 95 percent, Healer at 94 percent, Friend at 93 percent, and both Liberator and Help at 91 percent. The participants were able to check as many images of God as they felt relevant. One way of construing these images is to conclude that they represent God as Presence, which not only offsets the existential loneliness of persons, but also gives to persons good gifts that are valuable and eternally enduring. Certain life-giving themes emerge from these most frequently chosen images.

Creator God gives Purpose
Spirit God gives Freedom
Wisdom God gives Revelation
Friend God gives Nurture
Healer God gives Forgiveness and Restoration
Liberator God gives Power
Helper God gives Strength and Courage

In the 1985 study, an overwhelming majority checked the image of God as Creator. In 1992, Creator God and Spirit God tied for first place. The emergent themes of purpose and freedom tie these two together.

In creation, God's purpose for one's life is limitless and not to be circumscribed by human assignment. Rather, God has the freedom in creating any woman to invest her with gifts and callings that are unlimited and unchallengeable. "It is God that made us, and we are God's" (Ps. 100:3). Certainly no human being can say for sure what purpose each man or woman is called to fulfill. This belief about God grants freedom of being and expression that no human hierarchy can dismantle. With God all things are possible. It is God's prerogative to choose and appoint whomever God wills, irrespective of gender, race, or class. This strengthens the assertion on the part of women that it is God who called them. What person can, with certainty, question another's calling? This applies equally to male ministers. If we can limit God's choice in any way, it sets the stage for someone else to challenge whether or not God has called anyone, male or female. The essential issue is one of God's freedom and the free will given to all human beings by God.

The second number-one image of God selected was that of Spirit. "Now the Lord is the Spirit, and where the Spirit of the Lord is, there is freedom" (2 Cor. 3:17). Historically, black women have fared better and gained far more acceptance in those churches that stress the free flowing movement of the Holy Spirit. Such openness builds upon the belief that it is the Spirit that animates and then uses the man or woman of God, not the person alone. Therefore, what is required is a willing, yielding, obedient, righteous vessel. In religious communities where these are higher principles than the principle of gender, followers acknowledge the free movement of God's Spirit in anointing one for the mission, and giving the one the gifts necessary for the task. Both the passion and the competence for the work are from the Spirit, not from doctrine or education alone. Stress on the Holy Spirit allows for and invites innovation within worship and ministry. There is no set order that defies the possibility of God's doing a new thing. For many years, therefore, the largest acceptance of black women ministers was in certain Pentecostal and Holiness churches. These churches stressed the Spirit.

As a seminarian, in 1968 I documented that there were more black female pastors than black male pastors in the Shaw neighborhood of northwest Washington, D.C. I counted the many house and storefront churches that displayed the pastor's name as a female name. While these churches were much smaller than most of the churches pastored by men, their numerical count was higher (Causion Carpenter, 1968). The power to carry on these community-based ministries is almost always attributed to the assurance that the Holy Spirit is with them. They preach, minister, and evangelize, frequently in spite of the stigma and scorn of public opinion, because of the freedom of the Spirit. The Spirit authenticates their charisma as God-given and themselves as God-sent. As a young girl, I observed my grandmother participating with groups of black women ministers who aligned themselves with Women Ministers Alliances, a network along the East Coast from Washington, D.C., to New York. Later as a youthful preacher, I often ministered in their storefront churches, where grandchildren and other family members gathered to sing, pray, raise an offering, and hear the word of God delivered by women ministers. They supported each other, fellowshipping together. They were tenacious, often spending enormous time and resources overcoming transportation and financial problems to dress in the proper attire and to ensure that the programs were beneficial to all concerned. Their goal was to help get the unsaved saved, starting with their own families and the individuals and families who lived near their churches.

These women's collectives had a life of their own, almost invisible to dominant religious circles. There was one exception, however. They were often called on by large churches and even government officials to offer prayer, since their prayers were almost always heartfelt and were believed to reach heaven. On rare occasions, one of them was asked to bring a Women's Day message at a large church. But more often, they went to the nursing homes and the hospitals with music and words of exhortation. Creator and Spirit meant freedom from constraint to respond to the call of God in their own way. They published religious tracts and took their ministry very seriously, irrespective of whether others took them seriously or not. They ministered in the tradition of nineteenth-century black preaching women such as Jarena Lee, Maria Stewart, and Lucy Smith (Carpenter, 1986a). They exemplified in the late twentieth century the four survival strategies suggested by Delores Williams in her book *Sisters in the Wilderness:* "(1) an art of cunning, (2) an art of encounter, (3) an art of care, and (4) an art of connecting" (Williams, 1993). When women ministers could not be ordained elsewhere, these groups organized themselves and held ordinations. A number of large Baptist Ministers Conferences would label such ordinations "clandestine."

The attributes of God that rated highly or "much of the time" were *faithful, loving, forgiving, all-knowing, all-powerful, everywhere, close, understanding, dependable,* and *nurturing.* When "some of the time" responses were added, attributes such as *mysterious, transcendent, awesome, peaceful,* and *joyful* joined the list. Each of these attributes was checked in 90 percent or more of the responses. Of first importance seems to be the God who intersects with human need. Of second importance is the deistic, remote God. From these attributes, one can begin to outline certain constructs of thought related to the spirituality of black women.

It needs to be pointed out that Christian spirituality is much more than images and attributes of God. Spirituality is a given. It is not something separate from persons that has to be sought. It is who a person is in his or her deepest moments. Spirituality is a broad set of meanings including religious experiences. It is also a broad set of social psychological factors including religious biography, cognitive development, and personality. Spirituality relates to the inner, deep longing of the human spirit for a connection to, and a relationship with, God that can be experienced through an all-encompassing presence. The availability of these dynamics produces a process that integrates one's whole being and all of one's life experiences and life situations into a soulful center. Spirituality seeks the absolute fullness of creative love, found only in God.

Spirituality is a belief and hope that one can be a part of the habitation of God, a sanctuary for God, a touchstone. It is the part of a human being that invites the Holy Spirit with a welcoming reception. It emanates from an ontological center that moves on a continuum of equilibrium-disequilibrium. Several constructs are helpful in describing how the human spirit and Holy Spirit intersect. They are (1) order and purpose, which offers meaning, even that we are made in the image of God with a special purpose, (2) the guidance and instruction of scripture, reason, and tradition, which elicit the obedience that leads to a godly life, one filled with mercy, justice, and truth, (3) provision for protection from evil, which offers survival for life, and (4) worship and celebration, which offer a dwelling place for God's habitation among human beings, a place for the low-burning flame of peace and security.

Spirituality gives meaning, purpose, and perspective on how one sees oneself, others, and the world and how one organizes one's life.

Further, spirituality is a yearning to understand, to be understood, to belong, and to have inner peace.

While images and attributes of God do not constitute a totality of spirituality, they do reveal some of the concepts through which God is experienced. They give insight into the brokenness, recovery, and salvation that people of faith encounter on their human journey. Thus, they are important.

The listing below has been organized in such a way as to tie the most frequently selected attributes of God to various dimensions of spirituality that emerge from them.

Spirituality of Identity (all-knowing)
Spirituality of Survival (faithful, everywhere)
Spirituality of Relationship (close, loving, forgiving, nurturing)
Spirituality of Empowerment (all-powerful, understanding)
Spirituality of Mystery (mysterious, transcendent, awesome)
Spirituality of Celebration (peaceful, joyful)
Spirituality of Productivity (dependable)

We can compare the images of God with the dimensions of spirituality that emerge from the attributes of God. A pattern of conceptualization comes into focus accordingly. In this presentation, the image of God is related to a dimension of God. God gives to believers a quality that assures safety, security, meaningfulness, and significance.

Creator God gives purpose that leads to a spirituality of identity, which assures these women that God made them and knows all about them. Spirit God gives them the freedom to be whatever God has called them to be, which causes them to celebrate and count all their suffering as joy, for what they do is under the anointing of the Holy Spirit. Wisdom God gives them the revelation of the nature of God's holiness and salvation so that their spirituality consists of a special knowledge of God that informs their thinking and action. Although God is awesome and transcendent, they have been given a glimpse of God's mystery and glory. Friend God gives them the nurture to rely on their relationship with God, who is close, loving, and forgiving; thus, they are never alone. God is always with them, wishing them well even when family and others do not support them in ministry. Healer God gives them the recovery and salvation that they need when they are broken and weak, thus sustaining them in God's healing stream and renewing within them the good and ultimate intention that God has for them and their ministry. Since

God is faithful and everywhere, there is no circumstance, event, or feeling that is beyond the reach of God, and there is nothing that is too hard for God. They bounce back; they survive because of who God is. God is a good God all the time.

TABLE 11
Images of God Related to Spiritual Dimensions

IMAGE OF GOD ⟶	RELATES TO ⟶	DIMENSION OF SPIRITUALITY
Creator God	gives Purpose, which assures	Identity Order Vocation Obedience
Spirit God	gives Freedom, which assures	Celebration Unity Community
Wisdom God	gives Revelation, which assures	Mystery Reason Knowledge Intuition Discernment
Friend God	gives Nurture, which assures	Relationship Compassion
Healer God	gives Restoration, which assures	Survival Salvation Sustenance
Liberator God	gives Power, which assures	Empowerment Justice
Helper God	gives Strength, which assures	Productivity Courage Generativity Victory Fulfillment Completion

Liberator God gives them power to overcome adversity and accomplish the goals they set for themselves, whereby their spirituality is not timid or weak, but is one of empowerment. Helper God gives them the strength to endure whatever comes, until the victory is won and the assigned task is completed.

From the seven images of God and the fifteen attributes of God that rated highest among the female graduates, seven theological concepts can be postulated to form the core understanding of their spiritual power. They are *purpose, freedom, nurture, power, strength, revelation,* and *restoration.* Each of these can be explored more fully in later reflection upon both the quantitative and qualitative data of this study and others. These findings lend credence to womanist construction as a particularistic theology. The fact that these concepts parallel major topics within systematic theology in general hints at the potential universality of womanist theology. Womanists contend that they are for women, men, and community. Certainly, these seven themes would be life-giving for everyone. I remember a young, white, male undergraduate student saying that when he read Alice Walker's *In Search of Our Mothers' Gardens,* he thought, "That's me. This comes closer to reflecting what I believe than anything else I have ever read." He is now in graduate theological study. It will be interesting to observe whether or not his excitement about womanist theology persists as he reads a variety of other theologians.

Perceived Inhibitors of Ministerial Opportunity

These contemporary womanists "love struggle" (Walker). The eleven inhibitors of ministerial opportunity checked most often are listed below, according to the frequency of responses.

1. sexism
2. male clergy
3. racism
4. female laity
5. lack of leadership skills
6. weak interpersonal skills
7. lack of mentors
8. male laity
9. weak oratorical skills
10. lack of advocacy
11. lack of family support

Lack of acceptance inhibits the opportunity for women to use their gifts in service to others. If their acceptance is to be widened, each of the factors listed above must be probed, specific recommendations made, and, where possible, strategies adopted for overcoming them. Prior to this, however, there must be a greater understanding of the relationship between each of these factors and women ministers. More focused research is needed in this area.

Four of the inhibitors are gender-related: sexism, male clergy, female laity, and male laity. Sexism and male clergy were listed as the top two inhibitors in both the 1985 and 1992 studies. Sexism relates to institutional and historical factors that have led to discrimination against the equal treatment of women in the ministry. The item male clergy refers to the lack of support among male colleagues. This is disappointing, since male clergy are perceived as the power brokers of the American religious establishment.

The following observations were taken from telephone interviews with some of the participants. With regard to inhibitors to ministerial opportunity from black male clergy, one woman said, "They have stayed on the side. They were not in front for me." Another said, "Men need to promote black women in ministry. Preferably men need to push congregations to look for women in these positions (pastorates). They need a chance to get in the door." Another said, "We need honesty among male colleagues. They offer lip service to women, but withhold the training and support that could really empower women in ministry." One woman registered resentment against male clergy. She said, "Males go right into pastorates, not having to go the associate route."

Many of these women have to work in white environments, feeling especially rejected by black, male clergy. One woman said, "I had to leave the A.M.E. church. The male ministers are opposed to women." Another said, "In order to enhance our opportunities we need the brothers' support. Male leadership would be most helpful in improving things for women." The first ethnic woman ordained in her denomination said, "As a front-runner, the pressure and loneliness were incredible." She stated that she does not interact much with other clergy. She was told that she was ordained "to get a Ph.D. in religion, but not to pastor." She said, "Women have become honorary men."

One woman stated that she had no problem in her church. The parishioners did not like the authoritative style of the previous male pastor. A few women mentioned supportive husbands. In some such cases the husband was already retired when the woman entered the ministry. The divorce rate is high among those women who choose ministry after having been married for a number of years.

Male laity are perceived as much less of a problem than female laity. It is noteworthy that racism appears among the most-mentioned factors. It was listed by only a few of the women in the 1985 study. The fact that it surfaces in the 1992 study indicates that there is a great gulf to be overcome in American religion. The majority of positions in white denominations are reserved for the white clergy. Only a few slots are open to African American candidates. White churches still call white ministers, and likewise, black churches call black ministers, with few exceptions. Thus, the American church is still thoroughly segregated. Earlier in this century, Mahatma Gandhi challenged Howard Thurman in this regard. There seems to be a deep-seated need for American churches to remain ethnically homogeneous. This may be because of the pressures of a racist society in which blacks and whites are not yet at ease with one another. As most recent surveys have shown, though blacks and whites work together, they are still neighborhoods apart in social terms. They do not socialize outside the job, and they do not worship together on a regular basis.

Black churches, and probably all churches, while teaching and preaching inclusivity, remain great cultural conservators. This is of critical importance to blacks. They want contemporary generations to have an immersion experience in their history and heritage. The church is the single most accessible institution that can fulfill this mission. It provides a corrective to the distorted presentation of black culture that is portrayed in other parts of society, for example, in places of employment and in the media. In the African American church, blacks can still have one foot in America and one foot in the pride and dignity of racial consciousness, which the former does not consistently evoke.

Racism also causes the segregated housing patterns that result from white flight whenever neighborhoods start attracting more blacks and other racial/ethnic groups so as to render whites less than a comfortable majority. Whites still do not believe that blacks can sustain stable, safe neighborhoods. As soon as the neighborhood starts becoming less than two-thirds white, whites start moving out, no matter how professional the class of blacks that move in. Whites are willing to commute long distances to work, to ensure that the neighborhoods in which they live are predominately white. The complexion of the schools is of primary interest to those who have school-aged children. As a result, we have witnessed the resegregation of American public schools. This phenomenon should not be interpreted as a failure in busing or educational strategies, but as a failure on the part of whites to trust their children's well-being to an environment that is other than overwhelmingly white. Thus, neighborhood churches tend to be segregated. For all the reasons cited above, the fact that 62 percent of these women are in predominately white denominations means that the number of positions open to them is relatively small.

Next in the list of inhibitors was female laity. This citation points to the need for more dialogue and coalitioning between female clergy and female laity. According to the highest ranked items in this study, female laity participate with male clergy in preventing the empowerment of female clergy. Part of this can be attributed to the fact that laywomen are so active in the church and usually on an unpaid basis. As ordained women ministers come into the mix, seeking pay for doing many of the same things that older laywomen have been doing without compensation for many years, tension can result. Another part of this can be explained by the adverse teaching of black male clergy. Many of the negative views that black laywomen hold were taught to them by male clergy to whom they looked for the proper interpretation of the scripture. Almost always these clergymen use negative interpretations of the biblical texts to substantiate their positions.

There is also the phenomenon of sexual politics in the black church. Laywomen derive satisfaction from an identification with a strong, powerful, and successful black male minister. For many of them, the minister is the highest-ranking male with whom they can have a close association. This association can become family-like, since active churchwomen gain considerable access to the pastor. The good pastor knows to affirm and compliment these women on a routine basis. There appears to be a need for this in the lives of female churchwomen, both married and unmarried. This tendency of black women to elevate the minister can turn black men away from the church. Black men may feel put down amid the high accolades paid the preacher. Because the male in the home may feel that he cannot compete with the pastor, an adversarial role toward church may develop. To offset this dynamic, a few black churches are teaching wives to reinforce their husbands' esteem by intentionally elevating their husbands instead of the preacher, including inviting them to attend church.

In addition to the special place that male clergy hold in the lives of female laity, the high ranking of the female laity as an inhibitor may relate to the higher expectations that persons have for support from those who are like them—in this case, the expectation of women supporting women. Frequently, these expectations are not met.

The female minister cannot fulfill some of the needs met by the male minister. In part, this is because of the sexist nature of any society that signals to women that they cannot be legitimized without the approval of men. As long as young-adult females are encouraged to seek husbands in order to make their lives complete, women will continue to measure their self-worth by standards other than their own. Laywomen need to analyze what male ministers contribute to their well-being and seek other avenues through which the same benefits can be derived. Another consideration that needs further work is the extent to which one's image of God and the emphasis upon all-male disciples allows the male minister to benefit from the relational aspects of faithful women who transfer their feelings toward God to the male minister, who is often the instrument through which God's nature and promises are proclaimed. It is hard to break this tradition. But if there is any merit in this line of reasoning, perhaps more emphasis can be placed upon the female images and attributes of God and the female biblical personalities to help balance these gender implications.

Regardless of these factors, one must admit that male clergy have learned how to compliment, recognize, and reward laywomen for their attentiveness to the male minister. I do not think that women ministers have discovered how to do this in such a way that similar benefits may accrue, and those who do it are not yet as skillful at it as their male counterparts, who swap techniques through the old-boy network on a regular basis. On a few rare occasions, I have been privy to such conversations among male clergy. Some of them learned such "stroking" behavior from their minister fathers. Much more training needs to be given to women in this regard if, in fact, it is a healthy attribute. If it proves to be pathological or crippling, it needs to be set aside, and the attention and energy of laywomen need to be directed elsewhere.

Consciousness-raising is a key ingredient to overcoming these barriers. Since the female laity are most numerous in the black church, they must become more aware of the power that they have and be solicited to use it on behalf of the female minister in the same way as they have used it on behalf of the male minister.

A few ladies in a large congregation went to the pastor and asked if they could provide the same helping, protecting assistance to the woman minister on staff that the men's security force provided to the male pastor. The pastor agreed, and at the next women's conference the women arranged similar security and transportation coverage for both their own female assistant minister and out-of-town female preachers. This is exciting to hear, because it is evidence of an awakened consciousness to the differential treatment of male and female ministers, both of whom may be serving in the same congregation. It is also a self-empowering act for women to affirm their own gender in like manner as for the opposite sex.

The female minister must work consistently to nurture her relationships with both female and male laity. A vacuum in the rules governing how boundaries are set in the female-male dynamic gets in the way of adequate bonding between the woman minister and both these groups. Only experience will teach both groups how to affirm and support one another in acceptable, nonsexual, and nonthreatening ways. What is comfortable and appropriate for the congregational context is only now being explored. How important are boy-girl relations in the church? Only time will adequately tell. However, the presence of women ministers adds complexity to such a discussion.

Before leaving this discussion of gender issues in the parish, one other issue that has surfaced in my own pastoral ministry is worthy of comment. To what extent do men feel comfortable discussing the full range of their experiences with women ministers? While a few men wholeheartedly embrace the woman pastor and take her into their innermost confidence, I have observed a good number of men who operate on the fringe of the faith community, unsure of how to relate to the woman pastor. I have observed also a closeness and level of comfort between men and male associate ministers, which I doubt I can achieve as a woman. Men in the church still like to have their male-only buddy sessions as special occasions of deep solidarity. This is not a negative thing. It only raises the issue of how women bond with their male parishioners if they are excluded from such sessions.

The church needs to foster more inclusive models of ministry that at times allow men and women to talk apart from one another, but at other times allow them to come together, to break down the barriers that exist between them. I propose a team ministry that incorporates both males and females in ministry as a necessity if the church is to meet the diverse needs of men and women, not to mention their increasingly pluralistic congregations and communities.

Black female M.Div. clergy need support systems that give them affirmation and reinforce their value. The lack of such support among family members who are still uncertain of what such women can accomplish is painful. In the case of married clergy, it is difficult for the minister-wife to receive the same support that the minister-husband receives. Most male-female relationships have cemented around the female's reinforcing the male in his career achievements.

The fact that the woman's career development needs the same support is often missed. Females can become emotionally depleted from the demands of both family and those who depend upon her for ministry. Rarely are members of the congregation sensitive to her role as dual and triple caregiver. The only remedy is for women to learn how to ask for the help that they need. Congregations and, specifically, female laity who traditionally give this service to others need to be taught the differential caregiving demands upon female ministers.

An examination of the central thesis of the book *Men Are from Mars, Women Are from Venus* may shed light upon this discussion (Gray). This very popular book asserts that men seek respect while women seek love. It would seem to follow, therefore, that men are more apt to give respect to other men and that women are more apt to give love to other women. This is because people of goodwill tend to give to others what they themselves want and expect. Men understand that it is important for a man to have respect. This includes guarding his good name as well as his status. When men confer respect upon another man, they are, in part, reinforcing their own entitlement to the same. It results in a greater sense of security, team spirit, and bonding. This bonding resides in understanding what is communicated to the other man. In other words, the men are saying to each other, "I've been there, and I understand how you feel when your knowledge or competency is disrespected." It was illuminating for me to hear of a church where the wife in the clergy couple team was always prepared and the husband was perceived as less so. A prominent member of the community who belonged to this church went to the husband and stated that the Mr. Reverend needed to get his act together, "because she (Mrs. Reverend) was always together." This gentleman felt uncomfortable with the wife being more organized and prepared than the husband. According to his worldview the opposite was to be true, and he sympathized with the brother whom he acknowledged as needing a high level of respect in the community.

African American clergymen have rushed to the defense of other black men out of this same sense of black male solidarity. One such incident was the public support that Mike Tyson received when charges of rape were made against him by a black sister. Tyson stayed in the home of one of the prominent ministers in the city where the incident occurred. The male ministers focused on the past injustices of the criminal justice system toward black males and on restoring dignity and respect to another black man, in this case Tyson. This appeared to be of more urgent concern to them than was the criminality of his behavior. The black clergymen demonstrated an insensitivity to the disappointing message that it was sending to the black women of America. Their initial concern was for black male solidarity.

Social and societal expectations are central to understanding gender differences. Human beings are greatly influenced by what they believe is expected of them. They define both themselves and how well they are doing (feelings of affirmation or their lack) accordingly. Gender expectations for males and females are still sufficiently differentiated within the culture of the United States. More is expected from men in the areas of ambition, status, and salary. Consequently, men usually have more intense ambitions for higher status and salaries than do women. This explains why girls who do well initially in all academic subjects in school eventually lower their expectations of themselves and thus their achievement in certain subjects, such as science and math. They have received a message through their socialization as females that achievement in these areas on their part is neither expected nor appreciated. This may also parallel the erosion of their self-esteem. To admit to the fact that males are supposed to know certain things and be better at certain things than females is to acknowledge that men are better than women relative to status and economic achievement. There are other areas where women are supposed to surpass men. These include compassion, nurture, and moral rectitude, none of which seem to have economic or political currency.

This same foundational theory of gender roles partially explains why men and women will often say that it is women who are more opposed to women ministers than men. Upon examination of the truth of such a statement, one has to factor in the role that female expectation is playing. Women do not respect women in the same way that men or women respect men. They are unclear as to why women need or should be given more respect than they themselves expect to receive. They will say, "She's the same as me." The women are more likely to call a black female clergywoman by her first name, without any title given. While men confer on one another what they wish to receive, women confer on women what a still-patriarchal culture has taught them that they need to receive and give. It is a matter of the golden rule, that is, "Do unto others as you expect them to do unto you." Thus, gender expectations are an important part of this issue.

This presents a dilemma for the female pastor. If she stands and demands the same respect she sees men demanding and receiving, she is branded unladylike and immodest. The women in her congregation want her to be satisfied with just knowing that they love her. They want her to show humility and to be long-suffering and patient. But when a woman is not given the same authority as men in the same office of pastor, there is an erosion of her effectiveness as a leader and her ability to get things done organizationally. She may still have the personal connections for good and even excellent one-on-one or small-group support, but her corporate leadership is diminished. Both men and women expect her to be more forgiving and kinder in dealing with challenges to her authority than a man would be. If the problem is with a male leader, the male may be protected and conceded to because he is in the minority in the church. Men are known to get upset with the preacher, go home, and never return to church again. If he is responsible for the care and upgrading of the church property or for the church finances, it is all the more critical that the woman pastor's issues be overlooked. The women in the church want the female minister to honor this, because she is supposed to be able to understand. And the worst case scenario comes when people say, "She brought it on herself."

The whole church could benefit from laywomen's becoming more sensitive to the needs of female church leaders, both clergy and lay. Black women ministers could accomplish a great deal if they showed interest in and solidarity with their lay sisters in the congregations. There is much to be done in this area, beginning with consciousness-raising and then moving on to sisterhood.

Perceived Promoters of Ministerial Opportunity

These contemporary womanists "love themselves. Regardless" (Walker). By design, the women were asked to identify the factors that they felt promoted the greater acceptance of themselves as ministers, and which would increase their ministerial opportunities. Promoters of ministerial opportunity were identified as:

1. completion of seminary
2. spiritual maturity
3. leadership ability
4. personal qualities
5. clergywomen

6. interpersonal skills
7. family support
8. oratorical skills

How can advocates promote wider acceptance and greater opportunity for women ministers? These women have identified some very specific factors. What is striking is that women are not looking to men to do it for them. Nor are they focusing upon the great "isms" that are beyond their control. They are focusing upon things that they can do. This represents a realization of the need for self-reliance. The things that matter most are education, personal qualities, spiritual maturity, and other women ministers. Seminary education rated most highly. It should be pointed out that until the 1970s, very few black ministers, male or female, received the M.Div. degree or its predecessor, the Bachelor of Divinity degree. The power of this credential in the legitimization of black women ministers is both intriguing and encouraging.

Personal qualities remain high as both inhibitors and promoters in both the 1985 and 1992 studies. In the 1992 study, personal qualities rated 69–79 percent on the promoting side, and 46–57 percent on the inhibiting side. There is a danger here. It may be overly optimistic for these women to attribute so much of their own successes or lack thereof to personal qualities. This could lead to a sense of failure if they do not gain the acceptance and positions they feel they are deserving of as time goes by. They could become inappropriately frustrated in the face of inhibitors and promoters that are beyond their control.

Oratorical skill was rated highly both as an inhibitor and as a promoter. This is an acknowledgment that prowess in the pulpit is an elemental key for acceptance in the pulpit. This points to the need for a variety of positive female preaching role models. They also need to hear as many different styles of feminine preaching as possible. Women do not generally have the low or loud voices to which most parishioners have become accustomed. This often discourages women. Many have feelings of inadequacy regarding their style of sermon delivery, even when their content is exemplary. In the seminaries, there is a need for female preaching instructors to give greater affirmation to the prowess of female speakers. Every woman minister needs to work in this area to be more in touch with what is most effective for her. In my opinion, it is regrettable when one hears that a woman minister's role model for preaching was a man. Yet such is frequently the case. It is difficult for women to match the style and delivery of male preaching. I know that I cannot compete with men who require no voice amplification. I marvel at how some of them can come down into the aisles without the assistance of a microphone. When I reminded one parishioner that I always needed a microphone when I moved out of the pulpit, she said, "That's all right, we all know you're a girl." I laughed as I realized that most people are aware of this. I'm not sure that most women ministers can take consolation in this. Even those who pastor large numbers of congregants comment on the favor that the male vocal instrument can stir in the church. Comments range from "soothing" to "sexy." Preaching is letting God use one's personality, mind, voice, and body. Each woman called by God has been given all that is necessary and should strive to use all her gifts naturally. It is a turnoff for men and women alike to hear a woman trying to preach like a man. It is also distracting to hear a man or woman using so much affectation in their speech and presentation that it sounds and appears artificially imposed rather than a natural extension of their own personality and conversational tone. There is much more sincerity emitted when the audience hears the real person coming through. The audience wants to first meet the person who is used by God. Of course, there are exceptions to this. Some persons I've known admire and prefer the male "preacher" sound. Since Rev. Martin Luther King, Jr., made it world famous, it has been acclaimed and used not only by black preachers, but also by more and more black politicians and attorneys.

Finally, in the preaching act and its preparation, what makes the critical difference is the anointing of God, which gives the preacher the passion and excitement that sets the hearers' faith response on fire. It's not achieved in voice lessons or dramatic recitation. It is in waiting on the Lord to give one a true word that is so ready for delivery that it must come forth. A simple prayer for the power to be persuasive and clear in one's delivery is critical. Some types of sermons work better in the hands of certain preachers. Preaching is both a craft and an art. When creative expression joins hands with careful exegesis, grounded in real experience and storytelling, black preaching emerges as the testimony of a yielded vessel, honored by God to proclaim God's purpose and God's will in history.

Esther

Esther is a Tennessee woman who was ordained a United Methodist deacon in 1979 and an elder in 1984. She is married, and her husband is a state government employee. Sometimes his career has prevented her career advancement, and sometimes her career has interfered with her husband's career advancement. Esther's husband shares in the housecleaning, cooking, and getting the children ready for school. Their children are ages 11, 12, and 16. This dual career couple has not worked in the same geographic area for the past six years. Esther is a full-time, salaried pastor who earns $20,000–$29,000 a year. She pastors three small churches that have a combined membership of 150. Two of the churches are growing, while one is "static." Esther has been pastoring churches for the past twelve years. When asked if she finds her M.Div. education helpful, she said, "I guess I'm using it," but she adds that she has had "very few opportunities" to gain experience since seminary. One of the places where her education is used is on a denominational leadership team for spiritual formation. In this capacity she gets to address African and African American spirituality.

Regarding her acceptance as a woman pastor, Esther has faced some opposition. At the denominational level of district superintendent, bishop, and other clergy, some have been accepting of her and some have not, she said. As a United Methodist, she is under the itinerant appointment system and admits, "I did not accept an appointment. That has inhibited me from getting a more challenging appointment." She feels her career is considered second-class when compared to male M.Div. graduates.

Most of Esther's interaction with other clergy is at district clergy meetings. She has been part of two support groups, one for clergypersons and one for clergywomen, but at present, she is not an active member of either group. She currently has no mentor, but when she did, they met once a month. She admits that she has not been mentoring other women.

Male participation in Esther's churches is "very low," and she believes that men need more encouragement than women to participate in church. She has given extensive community service, serving as president of the NAACP and sitting on the board of directors of a local day-care center and adult learning center. She also challenges other people to be active both in the local church and in the community. In her leisure time, Esther reads and listens to music and plays the piano. Given an opportunity for gaining greater competency in ministry through continuing education, she would pursue a degree in pastoral counseling. She is in the process of applying to a Ph.D. program. Her most effective gifts for ministry are in pastoral counseling and liturgy.

Esther feels that the system she is in is in need of change. Although there are strategies on paper to improve it, it is not actually happening. The church system, in her view, is not inclusive, and women pastors need more challenging positions. What sustains her through these challenges are prayer and daily devotions. Her favorite theological image is "being rooted and grounded," being reminded that Jesus is the "Root of Jesse." Most often she portrays God as just and gracious, and her most cherished image of Christ is of him speaking with the woman at the well. Here Christ demonstrates that he is inclusive of people who are different. Jesus gave the woman at the well a message, and she carried the word. Esther worries that a larger percentage of women are preparing for a church system that is not ready to include them. She said women are viewed as "last-class, not even second-class" within the church. She perceives a hierarchy where white clergymen come first, white women come second, black clergymen come third, and black clergywomen come last.

Clearly, this woman has identified the problems of both sexism and racism. She has also pointed to the difficulty of dual-career couples. After twelve years, her experience in pastoring does not seem to be challenging. She would like to see black clergywomen placed in more challenging situations. She is an example of highly educated women who are being placed in small, unchallenging situations with nowhere else to go. Fortunately, she is able to serve on denominational task forces and community boards that use her expertise, but this is usually without compensation. Most clergywomen do not have this luxury, and when they do, they often find this pattern of work for no pay to be exploitative.

Before becoming a pastor, I used all the vacation time from my job as a college administrator to travel to church-related meetings as a resource person. I was never compensated for this activity. Once, an executive of a major philanthropic foundation informed me that I had been an adviser on an unprecedented number of their grants to religious organizations, more than any other consultant. He noted that he thought I had never been adequately compensated for these services, whereupon he proceeded to offer me a lucrative contract that continued for three years. Although I was greatly appreciative, this scenario is rare for most women. More frequently I observe seminary-trained women who give enormous numbers of hours and years in regional and national church deliberation, and only occasionally does such activity translate into salaried positions.

Once, as a student, when I conducted a large regional survey on the needs of women in our denomination, my professor who reviewed the statistical work asked if I was being paid for my services. When I answered, "No," he remarked, "The church is the most exploitative institution I know." Understandably, the church is a volunteer organization, but why should persons who have been professionally trained to give leadership to the church, and who do not have another profession that will pay them on a professional basis, have to render service uncompensated? One pastor friend told me that she used to perform weddings free of charge until her associate informed her that he was paid $300 to sing two or three solos per wedding. He suggested that her services were even more valuable than his. He said, "Why not ask for more pay?" and she did. The notion that ministers should not be paid for their services comes to us from the Catholic vows of poverty for the priesthood and from a time when black ministers were not professionally trained. In the former case, the Catholic church provides amenities and care for its priests, which the black Protestant church has never done. And now that black clergy are professionally trained, both men and women should be paid on a level commensurate with their training.

The "rooted and grounded" image of God is very reminiscent of my grandmother's spirituality, which is illustrated in the song "I Shall Not Be Moved." The song says, "Like a tree planted by the water, I shall not be moved." It declares that the singer has a determination to triumph over adversity. Nothing will be able to take Esther away from the place where God has called and planted her. Regardless of the measure of human success that she feels, there remains the need to be faithful over the things entrusted to her hands.

There is a quality of staying power here that sustains this woman, as it did my grandmother, even in the face of adversity. Thus, black women have certainly been among the called, the chosen, and the faithful.

6

Learned African American Clergywomen at the Beginning of the Twenty-first Century

Based upon demographic data collected from black women ministers around the country, a composite profile can be derived that embodies the typical black woman pastor. Let us call her Mary, which is a fictitious name. She embodies the average or most common traits found in the women pastors who responded to a 1999 study. Pastor Mary is a single mom in her forties who lives in Maryland and serves a United Methodist church. Her salary is in the $20,000 range. She is divorced and has two children. Mary was thirty-nine years old when she entered seminary, and she graduated in 1992. She is now in her forties. She has had two male mentors; one was her pastor and the other was a friend. She feels accepted as a minister.

There are two items here that are troubling. The first is the low wages. Given her three years of graduate education and their cost to her, this seems to be a small return on her investment. One would conclude that she does not have monetary gain as an objective. In addition, there are probably huge responsibilities placed on her as a single mother who is a primary caretaker and provider. It is only her faith that sustains her; she believes that God is with her to strengthen her. She has been highly educated, but receives little compensation. However, she values the sense of peace and purpose that springs from her spirituality. American society has been described as narcissistic and materialistic, but her focus is on spreading the gospel of Jesus Christ and serving others.

Although there are certain clergy tax advantages that may help her financially, these advantages are offset by the probability that she does not receive the customary benefits package. In most cases, companies or institutions offer approximately 26 percent in benefits on top of the designated salary. Because ministers are self-employed, such items as health insurance, pension, and annuity must be subtracted from their salary packages, thereby reducing their consumable income. For example, if a clergyperson earns $30,000, he or she may have to subtract 14 percent for pension ($4,200) plus another $4,500 for family health insurance. In this manner, the $30,000 is reduced to $21,300. If an annuity plan or dental plan is added, the salary becomes even lower.

How are seminary-trained black women doing as a professional group? A survey of 324 of them discovered some important positive indicators of their success in the ministry. Ninety-four percent of the women felt accepted, liked, and appreciated in their ministry positions. Comparing where the congregation was when they arrived with where the congregation is now, there is an increase in the number who indicated growing and developing–from 40 percent to 64 percent. The generally declining response fell from 28 percent to 13 percent, lower than half. It is healthy that these women perceive that the congregations they serve have improved since they arrived. This is also an excellent point for those skeptical of the ability of women to lead churches toward vitality and renewal. As one postal executive expressed the risk factor in hiring a woman pastor, he said, "I don't blame the churches for not wanting to hire a woman. They know what a man can do in the job, but they are not sure of what a woman can do." At least according to the women themselves, their leadership is resulting in churches that are growing and developing. This explains why 90 percent felt that they were accomplishing things.

Ninety-five percent felt joy from their work. Eighty-nine percent have been successful in overcoming difficulties in their ministries. Eighty-seven percent have been able to maintain separation between their ministerial duties and their family duties. Ninety-two percent felt spiritually whole and that they were growing in spiritual depth.

Ninety-four percent felt physically healthy and energetic. Ninety-six percent were assertive on issues of justice for others. Eighty-nine percent were assertive in obtaining justice for themselves. Overall, therefore, these women are faring well in the areas mentioned thus far. However, their portrait is not without some formidable problems and struggles. The women themselves attest to sizeable dissatisfaction. When asked the overall level of satisfaction that they experience in their ministerial career, only 44 percent indicated excellent or good; 56 percent, more than half, expressed fair or poor satisfaction. This chapter tries to give a balanced view of life among contemporary black clergywomen relative to their male counterparts.

Methodology

This data was collected in the summer and fall of 1999. The participants included both male and female Master of Divinity (M.Div.) graduates. Potential respondents were identified with the help of the Association of Theological Schools (ATS), which provided the names of member schools that had enrolled African American M.Div. students between 1972 and 1998. A letter requesting the names was sent to the executive officer of each school. A sixteen-page questionnaire was sent to each name submitted. Not every school responded, but the majority did. In a few cases, the schools would not release the information, but members of their staff sent the questionnaires to their graduates. The results come from an analysis of the returned questionnaires. There were 3,117 question-naires mailed, and 800 were completed and analyzed. The sample includes 476 males (60 percent) and 324 females (40 percent). The respondents are from eighteen different denominations and from sixty-one different seminaries.

This is a return rate of 26 percent, which is a lower than the return rate in two previous studies. The return rate of the 1985 study was 39 percent, and the return rate of the 1992 study was 34 percent. There are two explanations that may, in part, account for a lower return rate in 1999. First, in 1985 and 1992 only female M.Div. graduates were surveyed. It may be that men did not return the questionnaire in the same proportion as women, since the research is mainly focused on women. Second, this was the third time a number of the same women were contacted, being asked essentially the same questions. Some of the women may have thought it redundant.

In the previous chapter, a general profile of black female seminary graduates emerged as a reflection of their progress in the ministry. That chapter examined and interpreted their perceived sources of power to prevail in the ministry, even when the negative forces seem to outweigh the positive. Current data is presented in this chapter that either reinforces or refutes earlier studies. After seven more years, between 1992 and 1999, new patterns of advancement and retrenchment are apparent. The new study included both men and women, but in this chapter the focus is on the 324 women who responded. This sample includes over one hundred more black clergywomen than the 1992 study of 203 women.

Graduate Theological Schools

Eighty-three percent of the 324 women were graduated from eighteen different seminaries nationwide. Howard University graduates are the most represented with 23 percent of the total. The Interdenominational Theological Center and Virginia Union University School of Theology graduates account for 12 percent and 11 percent respectively. Other schools with ten or more graduates in the sample are Duke University Divinity School, New York Theological Seminary, Princeton Theological Seminary, Wesley Theological Seminary, and Shaw University Divinity School.

Some of the institutions that graduate considerable numbers of African Americans in the M.Div. degree are not included. Hopefully schools such as Harvard University School of Divinity, Boston University School of Divinity, Hood College, and Payne Theological Seminary will participate in the future. In one case, the names and addresses were received too late for inclusion in this chapter.

Age

The ages of these women ranged from twenty-five years old to eight-one years old. The median age was fifty. Sixty-one percent were in their forties and fifties. Only 1 percent were in their twenties, and 10 percent were in their thirties. This is an older population than the ones reported in 1985 or 1992.

Ordination

The number of women who were ordained rose from 76 percent in 1985 to 90 percent in 1992. In 1999, 80 percent of the women were ordained compared to 93 percent of the men. This represents a proportionate decline of 10 percent since 1992. The denominations in which the most women were ordained were United Methodist (15 percent), A.M.E. (13 percent), American Baptist (10 percent), National Baptist (7 percent), and Missionary Baptist (5 percent).

TABLE 12
Ages of Respondents

Ages of Respondents	Birth Year of Respondents	Percent of Respondents in Each Age Group	Number of Respondents in Each Age Group
80s	1910–1919	1	2
70s	1920–1929	4	11
60s	1930–1939	13	40
50s	1940–1949	34	105
40s	1950–1959	37	116
30s	1960–1969	10	34
20s	1970–1979	1	5

Age at Ordination by Gender

The median age of these women when they entered seminary was forty years old, and the median age at ordination was forty-three. The age at ordination for men was sixteen to sixty years old; for women it was eighteen to seventy. There is a major difference in the age distribution by gender. Two-thirds of the men (66 percent) compared to one-fourth of the women (27 percent) were ordained by thirty-five years old. More than three times as many women (37 percent) as men (11 percent) were ordained after they were forty-five years old. While 17 percent of men were ordained by age twenty-five, only 4 percent of women seem to have gone directly from college to seminary to ordination. The majority of men are under thirty-five; the majority of women are under forty-five. One-fourth of the women were ordained between the ages forty-six to fifty-five, at a much later age than the men.

Entering the ministry in later years of age can be a liability for women in two ways. First, most traditional churches, when seeking a pastor, generally favor a young man thirty-five years old and younger. One prominent urban pastor served one church for fifty years, half a century. He went there when he was twenty-four years old. Young male graduates are called to pastor in their twenties, in contrast to women who are completing seminary in their mid-forties. The problem with women beginning ministry at age forty-five or later is that once they serve their first church, in approximately five years they may not be invited to apply for another congregation. In this way they do not get the opportunity to learn from their early mistakes and to benefit from a fresh start somewhere else. It is very difficult for women to become first-time pastors after they reach fifty years old. When they do, these older women are relegated to smaller churches.

With regard to ordination by denomination, there is a considerable difference between black men and women. Fifty-two percent of the men in the historic black denominations were ordained; only 35 percent of the women were ordained. There was not so great a gender difference between ordained men and women in the white mainline denominations. Thirty percent of the sample were ordained African American men in white denominations. The percentage of black women in white denominations was higher than the percentage of black men in those denominations. Conversely, there was a larger percentage of ordained men in the black denominations.

Among those thirty-one women who were not ordained, 58 percent finished seminary after 1997. While some graduates are ordained immediately after completing seminary, it is not unusual for ministers to postpone the ordination process until they have completed their studies. This is especially true when seminarians switch denominations. There can be different or extra requirements that delay their ordination. One of the most time-consuming requirements is clinical pastoral education. If this clinical training is not completed during seminary, the large number of hours required per week is a hardship for persons who must work full-time to support themselves. If graduates switch denominations, their ordination requirements may include the history and polity of the new denomination. Therefore, it is not unreasonable that 20 percent of the female graduates are not ordained, given that more than half of them had graduated during the last three years covered in the study (1997–1999). Half of these unordained women are in the National Baptist (16 percent), American Baptist (16 percent), and Presbyterian (19 percent) denominations.

Ordination by Denomination and Gender

The largest differences in the numbers of men and women ordained by denomination were found in the American Baptist (5 percent male, 10 percent female), Missionary Baptist (11 percent male, 5 percent female), and National Baptist (20 percent male, 7 percent female). One wonders how many of the Missionary and National Baptist women switched to American Baptist for ordination purposes. The American Baptist was 2 to 1 female; the Missionary Baptist was 2 to 1 male; and the National Baptist was 3 to 1 male. It has become commonplace for black Baptist congregations to be dually aligned with the American Baptist Conference. The dual affiliation of the Missionary and National Baptist with the American Baptist raises the possibility of legitimizing the ordination of women. Thereby, a local congregation can ordain women through their American Baptist affiliation without jeopardizing their fellowship with the other prohibitive denominations. None of the fourteen Church of God in Christ (C.O.G.I.C.) ordained ministers in this study were women. Although a few C.O.G.I.C. bishops permit it, the stance of the national church is prohibitive.

Present Denominations

Between 1992 and 1999, the American Baptists stayed steady with 10 percent women in the sample. The United Methodists, though still the largest group in the sample, fell from 22 percent to 15 percent; the Black Methodists rose slightly from 13 percent to 19 percent; the Black Baptists also rose from 13 percent to 16 percent; the Presbyterians dropped significantly from 11 percent to 2 percent. The other white mainline churches account for 11 percent, down from 17 percent. Whereas the 1992 sample was over 61 percent white mainline, the 1999 study is only 40 percent white mainline. This is probably due to the slight increase in opportunity in the black denominations, especially the A.M.E. church. The black denominations weigh in with 35 percent, up from 26 percent in 1992.

Fifty-six percent of the women were brought up in the historic black denominations. The National Baptist and Missionary Baptist led the way with a combined 36 percent. Presently, 36 percent of the women remain in the seven historically black denominations. This is an overall loss of 20 percent, which is more than the 16 percent loss among those who had shifted denominations in 1992.

The 36 percent who remain are primarily in the A.M.E. (11 percent) and National Baptist (8 percent). Women are switching denominations more than before.

TABLE 13
Denominations of Origin

DENOMINATIONS			
Historic Black	Combined Male & Female	Male	Female
A.M.E.	9%	9%	9%
A.M.E. Zion	3	2	3
C.M.E.	3	3	3
C.O.G.I.C.	3	4	1
Missionary Baptist	16	15	17
National Baptist	22	24	19
Progressive National Baptist	4	3	4
Total	**60%**	**60%**	**56%**
Mainline White			
American Baptist	6%	4%	8%
Disciples of Christ	2	3	2
Episcopalian	3	4	2
Lutheran	3	5	1
Presbyterian	3	2	3
U.C.C.	1	1	1
United Methodist	10	8	13
Total	**28%**	**27%**	**30%**
Southern Baptist	3%	3%	4%
Other	10	10	10

Most black people originated as Black Baptist—42 percent of the men and 40 percent of the women. Baptist is also where the greatest change is among both groups. The Missionary Baptists are down 9 percent. The National Baptists are down 10 percent. The women in the National Baptists are down 11 percent. The Progressive National Baptists added 5 percent male. In summary, switching denominations has resulted in 16 percent less black clergy as Black Baptists. The largest overall gain of 8 percent was made by the United Methodists.

The number of black women increased in the United Methodists by 9 percent, the American Baptists by 4 percent, and the Lutherans by 4 percent.

TABLE 14
Present Denominations

DENOMINATIONS		GREW UP IN	
Historic Black	Combined Male & Female	Male	Female
A.M.E.	10%	9%	11%
A.M.E. Zion	2	1	3
C.M.E.	2	3	2
C.O.G.I.C.	1	2	2
Missionary Baptist	7	8	5
National Baptist	12	14	8
Progressive National Baptist	7	8	5
Total	41%	45%	36%
Mainline White			
American Baptist	8%	6%	12%
Disciples of Christ	4	4	3
Episcopal	3	4	1
Lutheran	4	4	3
Presbyterian	5	4	6
U.C.C.	4	3	4
United Methodist	18	16	22
Total	46%	41%	51%
Southern Baptist	4%	5%	2%
Other	9	8	11

Switching Denominations

In the 1985 study, 51 percent of the women had switched from their denominations of origin during and after seminary. In 1992, 52 percent had switched denominations. However, only 27 percent switched during and after seminary. This was a major change in that 25 percent had switched before seminary. In 1999, 45 percent reported that they had switched denominations. This is a slight decrease but still represents a significant finding. Among those who changed denominations, 24 percent indicated that the change was ordination related. This usually means that they left their denomination of origin for another in order to become an ordained minister. Fifteen percent indicated that it was employment related. Among the factors listed as reasons for changing denominations, other than ordination and employment, marriage-related matters accounted for 22 percent of the other category.

It is interesting to note that men switch denominations in nearly the same proportion as women. More research needs to be done to ascertain the reasons why male clergy switch denominations.

TABLE 15
Salaries and Denominational Switching

Salary Range	Switched	Did Not Switch
Under $10,000	16%	16%
10,000–19,999	16%	12%
20,000–29,999	26%	23%
30,000–39,999	23%	17%
40,000 and over	19%	31%

Those who switched denominations experienced lower salaries. Eighty-one percent of those who switched earned under $40,000, while 68 percent of those who did not switch earned under $40,000. Among those who earn over $40,000, only 19 percent switched as compared with 31 percent who did not switch denominations. This is an economic argument for not switching. Some of the more subtle issues related to switching denomination are discussed in a previous chapter.

Theological Orientation

In response to the inquiry about their theological orientations, womanist led all other designations for women, at 13 percent in 1992. It is most remarkable that so many women chose womanist. It had risen even higher in 1999 to 25 percent. Evangelical also doubled from 9 percent to 18 percent. Traditional rose from 10 percent to 17 percent. Liberal and liberationist stayed the same at 12 percent and 11 percent, respectively. Only 2 percent chose feminist. The implications here are clear. Black women continue to identify strongly with theology from the perspective of black women. The rise in the popularity of evangelicalism in American religion is registered among black women. The upswing in traditional theology reinforces a return to more conservative fundamentalism in American religion. A significant portion of black women share these views. This may be due to the strong influence of the white right-wing evangelical movement in contemporary American Christianity. African Americans do not share the conservative political views of white evangelicals, but do share their centrality of scripture, biblical preaching, and born-again and spirit-filled delineations. Certain crossover religious personalities, such as Bishop T. D. Jakes, exposed large numbers of blacks to white evangelicals. A school such as Oral Roberts University has done the same. In the case of the latter, the unique emphasis upon the healing ministry of Rev. Oral Roberts, a white evangelical and fundamentalist, has attracted many blacks as both individuals and congregations. The ability of Oral Roberts University to help accredit local Bible colleges through an evangelical accrediting body has also been attractive to large black congregations who own and operate such schools.

Clergymen grouped around traditional, liberationist, evangelical, and liberal theological orientations. Clergywomen widened their circle to include and elevate womanists. Table 16 shows the results of those who indicated only one category.

TABLE 16
Theological Orientation

Position	Male	Female
Liberal	22%	15%
Traditional	30%	20%
Feminist	0%	2%
Liberationist	24%	13%
Womanist	1%	28%
Evangelical	23%	22%

Marital Status

Thirty-six percent of the female respondents in 1992 were married. This slightly increased over 1985 when 34 percent were married. In 1999, 45 percent were married. Again, there has been a substantial increase in the number of those who are married. One of the new phenomena created by the woman minister is the clergy couple, wherein both husband and wife are preachers. It is not uncommon for them to work together in the same church. Of the 104 in this sample who answered the question, 15 percent of the women are married to ministers. This is the largest single category recorded in the husband's occupation responses. The next highest category is engineer at 11 percent.

Twenty percent were divorced in 1992, up from a divorced rate of 14 percent in 1985. The divorce rate for 1999 is 23 percent, again an increase but not as much of an increase as between 1992 and 1985.

In the *Women of the Cloth* study, which mainly included white women, 55 percent of the women ministers were married and only 10 percent were divorced (Carroll, Hargrove, Lummis). The higher divorce rate and single-never-married rate among black women ministers parallels the marital profile of the African American population in general.

TABLE 17
Clergymen and Clergywomen Combined Current Marital Status by Denomination

Single, Never Married		Married, Never Divorced	
A.M.E.Z.	33%	Southern Baptist	77%
Disciples of Christ	22%	Episcopal	65%
Episcopal	20%	Lutheran	59%
American Baptist	19%	Church of God In Christ	55%
Church of God in Christ	18%	C.M.E.	53%
Presbyterian	17%	A.M.E.	52%
National Baptist	14%	Disciples of Christ	48%
United Methodist	14%	Missionary Baptist	48%
A.M.E.	13%	National Baptist	43%
Lutheran	11%	American Baptist	42%
Missionary Baptist	10%	United Methodist	40%
United Church of Christ	10%	Progressive National	35%
Progressive National	8%	United Church of Christ	35%
C.M.E.	5%	Presbyterian	31%
Southern Baptist	1%	A.M.E.Z.	27%
AVERAGE	**14%**	**AVERAGE**	**49%**

Divorced/Remarried	
United Church of Christ	28%
Missionary Baptist	26%
United Methodist	23%
C.M.E.	21%
A.M.E.Z.	20%
American Baptist	19%
A.M.E.	18%
Church of God in Christ	18%
National Baptist	17%
Presbyterian	17%
Progressive National	16%
Disciples of Christ	15%
Southern Baptist	13%
Lutheran	11%
Episcopal	10%
AVERAGE	**17%**

Divorced	
United Church of Christ	24%
Presbyterian	22%
A.M.E.Z.	20%
National Baptist	19%
United Methodist	17%
American Baptist	15%
Lutheran	15%
Progressive National	14%
C.M.E.	11%
A.M.E.	10%
Church of God in Christ	9%
Missionary Baptist	8%
Disciples of Christ	7%
Episcopal	5%
Southern Baptist	1%
AVERAGE	**13%**

Marriage Rate: Married/Remarried	
Southern Baptist	90%
Episcopal	75%
Missionary Baptist	74%
C.M.E.	74%
Church of God in Christ	73%
Lutheran	70%
United Church of Christ	63%
United Methodist	63%
Disciples of Christ	63%
American Baptist	61%
National Baptist	60%
Presbyterian	48%
A.M.E.Z.	47%
AVERAGE	**66%**

Singleness Rate: Single, Never Married & Divorced	
A.M.E.Z.	53%
Presbyterian	39%
American Baptist	34%
United Church of Christ	34%
National Baptist	33%
United Methodist	31%
Disciples of Christ	29%
Church of God in Christ	27%
Lutheran	26%
Episcopal	25%
A.M.E.	23%
Progressive National	22%
Missionary Baptist	18%
C.M.E.	16%
Southern Baptist	2%
AVERAGE	**27%**

The findings of 1992 revealed a relatively high singleness rate of 66 percent among the women. This is a very high proportion when compared with all of American society. The singleness rate includes single-never-married, divorced, separated, and widowed. For 1999, the singleness rate for women is lower at 55 percent. Almost two-thirds of the women have children. The median number of children is three.

Comparing this portrait of clergywomen to clergymen, there is evidence of a higher marriage rate for men (79 percent) and a lower singleness rate for men (20 percent). The divorce rate for clergymen is 7 percent, one-third of the female rate.

The highest married-never-divorced were Southern Baptist (77 percent), Episcopal (65 percent), and Lutheran (59 percent). These are predominately white denominations. Among predominately black denominations, the highest single-never-married were A.M.E. Zion, C.O.G.I.C., and National Baptist. The highest divorced are United Church of Christ (24 percent), Presbyterian (22 percent), and A.M.E. Zion (20 percent). The highest divorced-remarried were United Church of Christ (28 percent), Missionary Baptist (26 percent), and United Methodist (23 percent). Those with the highest singleness are A.M.E. Zion (53 percent), Presbyterian (39 percent), and American Baptist (34 percent).

Within the denominations discussed, the combined married rates, including those who remarried, is 66 percent. The combined single and divorced rate was 27 percent. The denominations with the highest combined married and remarried rate were Southern Baptist (90 percent) and Episcopal (75 percent).

The marital statuses of men and women were quite different. Twice as many women were single and never married (10 percent male, 22 percent female), while divorced men remarried at a higher rate (23 percent male, 13 percent female). A little over half the men were married and never divorced, as compared with almost a third of the women (56 percent male, 32 percent female). The singleness rate for men was 21 percent. The singleness rate for women was 55 percent. The percentage of divorced women was more than three times higher than divorced men (7 percent male, 23 percent female). This is an improvement in the marriage rate for women. In the 1992 study it was only one-third. In this 1999 study it is 45 percent, which is approaching half. This is encouraging, since there is a stereotype of women preachers being single and not remarried. This has led some women to believe that men will not marry a woman preacher. This is documented in William Meyers' *The Irresistible Urge to Preach.*

Geographic Accessibility

The 1992 and 1999 results on geographic location are about the same. These women lived in thirty states and as far away as Kenya, East Africa. However, the majority were located mainly on the East Coast and in Illinois, Ohio, and Texas. Accessibility to graduate theological education is a source of power for this emerging new leadership group. The three historically accredited, predominately black theological schools are located on the East Coast. The geographic locations of Howard University, Virginia Union University's Samuel Proctor School of Theology, and the Inter-denominational Theological Center parallels the states of residence for these women. In the 1999 group of women, the majority lived in the Maryland and Washington, D.C., area where Howard University and Wesley Seminary are located (25 percent); 8 percent live in Georgia where ITC is located; 11 percent live in Virginia where Virginia Union (Sam Proctor) is located. Other groups live in North Carolina, 7 percent; New York, 6 percent; and Ohio, 6 percent.

Positions in Ministry

These clergywomen had served the church in a wide variety of capacities in both paid and nonpaid positions. The three most common nonpaid roles in 1992 were guest speaker and preacher, member of regional boards, committees for denominations, and counselor. Between 1992 and 1999 there has been a change in unpaid positions for women. The number one position in 1999 was assistant pastor at 32 percent. Teacher in a church-related school was second at 19 percent. Guest speaker dropped to third place at 18 percent. New to the list of highly ranked are founder of ministry at 12 percent and pastor at 9 percent.

Four other areas accounted for 9 percent of the women. They are director of Christian education, hospital chaplain, evangelist, and consultant. It is evident that the churches have learned how to use the unpaid services of seminary-trained black clergywomen in areas for which they have specialized training more than ever before. This may mean that the resistance to their functioning under a male pastor has diminished.

Some women welcome the opportunity to use their ministerial gifts, regardless of the compensation. Not as many men pastor on an unpaid basis (7 percent), but 9 percent of women do. These may be small churches that they have founded or mission situations where children and single mothers who are served do not have the income to support a paid minister.

Some women ministers keep their day jobs as they serve in ministerial positions. This applies to second-career ministers who work full-time as they study and continue to do so until retirement and pension from their secular jobs. After periods of not having any position in ministry, it is a joy for some of them to be invited to use their graduate theological training. They may not be financially rewarded, but they are fulfilled in volunteer positions. One friend returned to teaching public school after more than ten years of trying to establish herself in a ministry-related position in the church. Now with a steady source of income again, she is delighted to work on a volunteer basis. She filled in as supply pastor when the pastor of her church died and moved on to a major office in the regional manifestation of her denomination. She grieved initially that she seemed to be back where she started before seminary, but as time has gone by, she is increasingly happy to be given recognition and respect in unpaid, ministerial responsibilities. Again, equitable salary has increasingly become the new frontier. As a voluntary organization, the church relies on unpaid services in large measure. In this study, seminary-trained women have held unpaid positions in higher proportions than seminary-trained men. They have served without compensation more than men in the following positions: teachers in church-related schools and preschools (19 percent female, 8 percent male), founders of their own churches and ministries (12 percent female, 5 percent male), evangelists (9 percent female, 4 percent male), assistant pastors (32 percent female, 25 percent male), and church administrators (6 percent female, 4 percent male).

Turning now to paid employment, the vast majority of the women studied in 1992 worked in ten areas of ministry, with guest speaking first on the list at 55 percent and pastor as second at 48 percent. Thirty-six percent had pastored full-time. This was more than triple the 11 percent who pastored full-time in 1985. Associate pastors were next at 36 percent. Counseling came next at 25 percent. This was a healthy increase over the 14 percent who were working in counseling in the 1985 study.

The 1999 data, which includes a larger sample, paints a less optimistic picture regarding these same positions. Looking only at full time, 21 percent have been pastors (sixty-nine women), 12 percent assistant pastors, 11 percent guest speakers, and 7 percent counselors.

One way that we assess the size of the churches that these women serve is to look at their weekly attendance. The median attendance was 100. This means that half of the women serve churches with an attendance of more than 100, and half serve in churches where the attendance is less. Another important indicator of congregational vitality is the annual budget of the congregation. The median budget of the churches where these women serve was $113,000.

When part-time positions are added to full-time positions, the percentages change to 41 percent guest speaker (down from 55 percent), 31 percent pastor (down from 48 percent), 12 percent assistant pastor (down from 36 percent), and 15 percent counseling (down from 25 percent). Reviewing the lists of job designations, it becomes clear that primary jobs for most of the women are in the nonchurch-related realm and their second jobs are in the church-related realm. This raises the issue of health concerns regarding women ministers being overextended from working two jobs and having chief responsibility for child rearing. They are working one paid "day" job, volunteering in nonpaid positions of major responsibility and leadership in the church, and fulfilling non-remunerative family duties. These black women ministers were working in other ministerial positions as consultant (15 percent), professor (8 percent), hospital chaplain (11 percent), church administrator (12 percent), campus minister (5 percent), and youth minister (6 percent). In all areas these figures represent a decline in paid positionality. There has been a slowing down in the advancement of black women ministers. The gains that were made in one seven-year period have begun to be reversed in another seven-year period.

The most obvious explanation would be that employment opportunities for these women are not keeping pace with the growing numbers of women who are completing seminary. One-third of these women were new graduates. They finished seminary between 1997 and 1999. The three most recent graduating classes comprised one-third of the female graduates over a twenty-seven-year period. The first third finished between 1972 and 1991—a twenty-year span; the second third finished between 1992 and 1996—a five-year span; and the final third in the next three-year span. The accelerated growth in the numbers of black women finishing seminary with an ordination degree (M. Div.) is phenomenal. But there is a deeper, less obvious issue. This demonstrates the resistance to social change, especially

in an environment that does not seriously advocate career opportunities, equity in job placement, and salaries for black clergywomen.
Since this environment is the domain of the church, it is impossible
to bring the scrutiny of governmental agencies to bear. Thus, the
constitutionalized tradition of separation of church and state is the
keystone that prevents this from ever becoming a public policy issue.

Change in church policy with regard to equity and parity
considerations could be initiated by lay members. The greatest hope
for advocacy is among black laywomen, because they are the largest
constituency in the black church. They could, if ever they wanted
to, control most of the budget. They give the most money to the
church. The second great hope is among sympathetic black men.
Unfortunately, it does not appear that such men yet have enough
leadership power to influence change in this situation. If they did,
black clergywomen would be further along. There is no doubt that
the latter is an emerging group that is seeking to be of assistance in
the cause, because they believe that sexism in the black church is
wrongfully present. The fact that these women are still having
difficulty being placed after seminary was illuminated by some of
the nonchurch jobs that they held. Some ordained, professionally
trained women in the study are working as secretaries and office
managers. Many work in nonchurch educational settings, and some
work for government agencies. These 1999 findings are very similar
to the 1992 findings. Some women have returned to their first-career
occupation after investing in three years of full-time study and
receiving low wages in a rather uneven ministerial career. Some
never left their preseminary job. They worked their way through
school, taking mainly night classes.

This makes for a very diverse set of backgrounds and skills. These
women may be realtors, social workers, psychotherapists, public
defenders, or nurses. Their other types of employment include
lawyer, accountant, director of a nonprofit agency, business owner,
computer consultant, IRS agent, audiologist, financial analyst, and
gynecologist. It is exciting to imagine how the black church may tap
into such a rich reservoir of theologically trained practitioners.
Certainly the black church is not without highly skilled leadership.

The challenge for church leaders is to harness and use such
multitalented women in the most appropriate ways. Pastors would
do well to affirm a team ministry that consists of a learning
community where ministerial associates come together to improve

TABLE 18
1999 Full-time Paid Employment

Position	Male	Female
Church Administrator	13%	6%
Director of Christian Education	2%	4%
Military Chaplain	5%	1%
Pastor	49%	21%
Assistant Pastor	14%	12%
Guest Speaker	12%	11%
Counselor	7%	7%
Professor	4%	3%
Youth Minister	4%	1%

1999 Part-time Paid Employment

Position	Male	Female
Church Administrator	2%	6%
Director of Christian Education	3%	10%
Military Chaplain	3%	2%
Pastor	13%	10%
Assistant Pastor	14%	19%
Guest Speaker	20%	30%
Counselor	7%	8%
Professor	11%	6%
Youth Minister	5%	5

the quality of services offered through the church. Many of these women may enjoy working in areas of ministry that the senior pastor neither enjoys nor is most competent in. Ministry in the twenty-first century will be a team effort. Competencies once sought outside the church may indeed now be found on the ministerial team, as well as in the congregation. This could greatly empower black congregations to undertake more comprehensive endeavors than ever before.

Turning now to gender differences in paid positionality, the comparison between the clergywomen and the clergymen in the study begins with an examination of full-time positions. These positions have been held by men and women since seminary.

Unlisted positions were held close to the same levels by both men and women or they were held by under 1 percent of the respondents.

The biggest difference between men and women in full-time paid employment is full-time pastors. The men dominated here by more than two to one (49 percent male, 21 percent female). With the exception of director of Christian education and counselor, men hold full-time ministry jobs to a larger extent than women. In full-time employment among men, there was a 3 percent or more lead in church administrator, pastor, military chaplain, and youth minister. Turning to part-time employment, women lead the men in every category except pastor, military chaplain, professor, and youth minister. Some of the difference can be accounted for by the fact that women take major responsibility for child rearing and family cohesion. Juggling family life and full-time ministry is a concern of women ministers. Part-time ministry, especially assistant pastor, is attractive to married women. It is interesting that 30 percent of women are paid guest speakers and only 20 percent of the men. Two explanations may be offered. First, more speakers are needed for Women's Day and women's retreat events. Second, perhaps the men are more heavily subscribed in full-time paid ministries and are less available for part-time guest speaking. The two exceptions to this would be revivals and services of fellowship where male pastors do pulpit exchange. This finding invites further research.

TABLE 19
1999 Paid Positions Not Previously Compared by Gender

POSITION	FULL-TIME		PART-TIME	
	Male	Female	Male	Female
Minister of Music	.4%	0	2%	1%
Global Missionary	.6%	.6%	.4%	.3%
Denominational Staff	6%	6%	41%	59%
Campus Minister	3%	2%	4%	3%
Hospital Chaplain	8%	7%	56%	44%
Prison Chaplain	4%	2%	2%	.6%
Founder of Own Church/Ministry	5%	6%	3%	3%
Missions Worker	.8%	.9%	.2%	.6%
Evangelist	3%	.6%	6%	4%
Consultant	5%	4%	7%	11%
Teacher in Church-Related School	6%	4%	6%	4%

Size and Budget of Churches by Gender

Differences in number by gender hiring were minor among local congregations. In churches with memberships under 500, women-hires of 88 percent exceeded men-hires by 1 percent. Among churches with 300 members, women-hires of 67 percent exceed men-hires by 4 percent in full- or part-time employment. In the 500–1,000-member church, men-hires of 10 percent exceeded women-hires by 1 percent. Thus, there was not much difference between the sizes of churches and the number of men and women employees.

The budgets of the churches ranged from $420 to $10 million for the women and $3,000 to $4 million for the men. Eight males (2 percent) and one female (1 percent) are employed in churches with budgets over $2 million. All other categories seem to be equally male and female. The majority of ministers in this study work in churches whose budgets are under $300,000. Neither the size nor the budget of the church seems to determine whether a woman has a better or worse chance of being employed. As demonstrated elsewhere in this study, the main difference and point of disparity is in the gender-preference for appointments to the positions of pastor and associate pastor.

Salaries

In 1992, 10 percent of the women were earning $10,000 or less, while 42 percent were earning $30,000 or more. When looking only at the primary job, in 1999, 16 percent earned under $10,000, and 45 percent earned $30,000 or more, with the median salary being between $30,000 and $35,000. Of course, when the family income of the married women is included, the figures improve. The median family income for this group is between $50,000 and $60,000. The family income ranges from under $30,000 for 15 percent of them to $80,000 or more for the upper 15 percent.

Only 52 percent of the women are presently employed in ministry-related positions. Looking only at income from ministry-related employment and excluding nonministry-related positions, in 1999, 18 percent of the women earned under $10,000, and 42 percent earned $40,000 or more. The high percentage of very low wages reflects the lower salaries paid for part-time ministerial work. Much of the under-$10,000 income is from second jobs that are ministerial. The majority of the women acquire their primary salary from secular jobs.

The *Washington Post* printed an article entitled "Clergy Pay Varies Widely, Survey Says" on September 16, 2000. It was interesting to note that the national average for the senior pastor's salary was $63,940; the associate/executive pastor's salary was $48,061; the religious education minister's salary was $48,338; the minister of music's salary was $50,824; the youth pastor's salary was $39,406; and the pastoral care minister's salary was $47,074. These figures are based upon information from the National Association of Church Business Administration in Richardson, Texas. There are regional and denominational differences. These figures include only salary and housing and exclude retirement, automobile expenses, insurance, convention expenses, and continuing education expenses. It is clear that the black women in this study, based upon the national norms cited above, are poorly paid.

Overall for persons with one job, 30 percent are earning $40,000 or more. Thirty percent earn from $30,000–39,999, 20 percent from $20,000–29,999, 11 percent from $10,000–19,999, and 10 percent earn under $10,000. Among those reporting more than one job (36 percent), 17 percent earn under $10,000 on their second job, 5 percent make 10,000–19,999, 5 percent earn in the $20,000 range, 4 percent earn in the $30,000 range, and 5 percent make $40,000 or more. On average, nontaxable clergy benefits are in the $15,000 or less range.

The black church has been notorious for not paying an adequate pension for its clergy. The author has personal knowledge of a pastor of a large congregation of a Missionary Baptist church who was retired without a pension and, as a consequence, had to live in subsidized housing for the elderly. He had pastored this large congregation for more than forty years.

Looking at gender comparisons, the largest differences in salary were at the $40,000 and over level. While 36 percent of men earned at this level, only 21 percent of women did. This is a salary gap of 15 percent in the highest range. *Clergy women: An Uphill Calling* accounted for a 9 percent salary gap between men and women when experience is taken into consideration. Very few African Americans were included in that study, but it appears that the gap between black clergymen and clergywomen is even wider. Second-job salaries are lower and do not show any significant salary gap between men and women.

The salaries reported here come from a mixture of ministry-related and nonministry-related types of jobs. In order to get an accurate measure of the salaries paid for the positions that are ministry-related, a separate analysis was done of the ministry-related jobs alone. One assumes that these figures reflect the earning power of the M.Div. degree.

The average salary earned by women from ministry-related jobs within the Job 1 response was between $20,000 and $29,999. Fifty percent of the seventy-nine ministry-related jobs pay between $20,000 and $40,000. More of the respondents (20 percent) make under $10,000 than those who make over $40,000 from ministry-related jobs. Compared to many other occupational groups, the ministry pays less, and far less than other professional groups. This may be one of the reasons that some denominations are having difficulty attracting ministers, particularly younger ones, and particularly males, who usually strive to be trained in areas that can support their families. This has become more of an issue now that wives and potential wives are more likely to be well-educated and to have their own careers and their own sources of income. Most men prefer to at least match the income of their wives. When the wife earns more than the husband, the husband may feel that he is not carrying his weight or fulfilling an equal share of the family's financial responsibility. In some cases marital strain results when he cannot compete with his wife's salary. The church as a whole needs to explore this problem further and develop new strategies for educating congregations about the cost of leadership in the twenty-first century. Small-sized congregations need to understand when they cannot afford a full-time minister. Some ministers need to be trained who are willing to be bivocational, that is, be willing to work another job in addition to pastoring a church. In the past, most black ministers have been bivocational. The acquisition of the M.Div. degree has traditionally brought with it the hope that the graduate would be called by larger churches that could afford an adequate salary so that the minister would not have to work in secular employment. Unless the salaries offered keep pace with the rising cost of living, this will be less and less true. The ministry-related salaries reported in this study appear to be alarmingly low. Divinity students who are second career frequently keep their secular jobs until retirement. Most graduates need to have an income of $60,000, but there are few churches that can pay this amount to a recent graduate.

There is an inequity between the family incomes of men and women.

TABLE 20
Family Income

	Male	Female
Under $50,000	33%	50%
$50,000–79,999	33%	28%
$80,000 and over	33%	21%

Half of the families of the women earn under $50,000, compared to one-third of the families of the men. One-third of male families earn $80,000 and over. Only 21 percent of female families earn this amount.

The survey permitted respondents to list two jobs. Historically, black clergy have often been bivocational. In this study, 38 percent of men and 35 percent of women indicated salary received from a second job. Of those who answered whether these jobs were ministry-related, half of the jobs were ministerial. Job 1 was 65 percent ministry-related for men and 54 percent ministry-related for women. Job 2 was 15 percent ministry-related for men and 20 percent ministry-related for women. It seems that when the clergy are working two jobs, the first job is more likely to be ministerial than the second job.

Problems within the Opportunity Structure

Another way of assessing the opportunities available to these women is to examine the number of inquiries that these women receive from local congregations to become a pastoral candidate. More than one-half of these women (59 percent female, 34 percent male) indicated that they had received no letters of invitation to become candidates for pastoral positions. Normally churches that are seeking a new pastor will invite recommended ministers to apply and preach as part of the search process. One Baptist church, after reviewing the applications that they received, invited twelve candidates to come and preach in their pulpit. The number of persons who are allowed to preach and be interviewed varies greatly. In some cases, the favored candidate will be carried through the entire process without comparison. If he or she is blessed, no competition will be necessary as that candidate is affirmed each step along the way. On the other hand, a church may settle on three or more finalists and want to interview each of them and hear each one preach. Sometimes this preaching is done in a neutral pulpit. Sometimes such preaching is done in the church that is searching for the new minister. When the preaching is in a neutral pulpit, usually members of the search committee attend and report back to the larger committee and the congregation.

Only 13 percent of the women have received one such request to be a pastoral candidate, 15 percent two requests, 5 percent three requests, and 9 percent four or more requests. Once placed, the struggle is extended to the issue of career mobility. According to these women, it is admittedly difficult to get another church position. Only 33 percent said it was easy; twice as many (67 percent) said it was difficult. Looking only at the very-difficult responses, 14 percent of the men compared to 30 percent of the women indicated very difficult. Conversely, 18 percent of the men and 8 percent of the women said very easy. Fifty-three percent reported having trouble with one or more lay leaders in the churches they pastor/attend. More than half (53 percent) felt bored and constrained by the limits of their church positions, resources, or people. More than half (51 percent) did not feel sufficiently compensated for their ministerial work. Fifty-five percent felt lonely and isolated. Thirty-one percent thought seriously about leaving church-related ministry for some other kind of work. Fifty-seven percent felt the need for confidential counseling. Fifty-nine percent felt that they did not have enough time to do what was expected of them by their families or spouses/partners. Seventy-two percent felt that they imposed unrealistic expectations on themselves. Factors such as these are real stressors that may contribute to the dissatisfaction that a good number of the women expressed about the ministry.

Support Groups

Pastors need pastors; and while judicatory, executive ministers are touted as pastors, there is often not a sufficient trust factor to allow one to confide in persons who are in a position to enhance or diminish one's career advancement. The clergy support group may be a better place for ministers to receive sympathy and good counsel during troubling times or in particularly complex situations. There are hundreds and sometimes thousands of parishioners, their families, neighbors, and friends who call upon the minister for advice and priestly involvement. The minister desires to know whether or not he or she is handling situations in the most faithful, efficient way, in a way that is congruent with the Christian gospel and high professional standards. Because ministers often operate in isolation without consultation or regular evaluation, support groups serve well as collegial places for learning and affirmation. Less than half (46 percent) were members of support groups. Forty-seven percent belonged to mixed gender groups. Thirty-five percent belonged to predominately male groups and 16 percent were members of predominately female groups. Seventy-six percent of the groups meet monthly and 24 percent meet weekly. The majority (63 percent) are denominationally based groups.

Clergywomen are slightly more likely to be members of clergy support groups (44 percent male, 50 percent female). The majority of women who belonged to such support groups belonged to mixed gender ones (45 percent). Sixteen percent belonged to predominately male groups and 39 percent belonged to predominately female groups. These groups are primarily denominationally based (61 percent). Thirty-nine percent are ecumenical. Most of them meet monthly. There is a need for female support groups across denominational lines. They would be less competitive and less threatening in that each woman's place in the denominational pecking order would not determine how she feels about herself or how she interacts in the group.

Career Goals

These 324 women were aspiring to perform in all categories of positions in ministry. This section only addresses those positions that at least 10 percent of the women checked. This means that at least 32 women checked the goals mentioned below. The respondents could indicate that the position was a career goal upon entering seminary, upon finishing seminary, currently, all of the above, or the above in several combinations. Table 21 reports on the combined "Ever" goals and the combined "Present" goals.

Most striking is the fact that in every category, present aspirations are lower and more realistic in light of what the positionality section of this chapter revealed. Looking at their current career goals, pastor remains the number one career goal at 32 percent. It is instructive that assistant pastor has fallen to 12 percent. This may be because some of the women have already held this position and hope for advancement. Surpassing the desire to become an assistant pastor are ambitions for guest speaker, professor, counselor, and founder of own ministry. Of moderate attraction are positions as consultant, evangelist, teacher in a church-related school, denominational staff,

TABLE 21
Career Goals

Position	Ever Goals	Present Goals
Pastor	56%	32%
Guest Speaker	22%	16%
Professor (Seminary or Religious Studies)	25%	13%
Counselor	23%	13%
Founder of Own Ministry	19%	13%
Assistant Pastor	37%	12%
Consultant	14%	10%
Evangelist	15%	7%
Teacher in Church-Related School	13%	6%
Denominational Staff	10%	6%
Hospital Chaplain	14%	5%
Director of Christian Education	20%	3%
Church Administrator	11%	3%

and hospital chaplain. Of lesser appeal are director of Christian education and church administrator. See chapter 5 for a discussion of professor as a career goal.

The largest decline is reflected in the director of Christian education position. After attending seminary and after graduation, this career goal slipped from 20 percent ever to only 3 percent currently. This same trend was documented in 1992.

The most conspicuous gender difference in career goals was in the area of pastor. While two-thirds of the women never had the pastorate as a goal, two-thirds of the men did. Parallel to this, two-thirds of the women aspired to be a director of Christian education at one time; almost two-thirds of men did not. Other areas to which women aspired more than men were church founder, guest speaker, and consultant. Entering seminary, more women than men had a counselor goal, but it equalized overall.

To replace the pastor goal, women have dreamed of other ministerial outlets, not sure what they are. Things such as guest speaker and consultant are relatively vague. Some women who make costly sacrifices never find that perfect placement in full-time ministry. Some are forced to follow ministry as an avocation while returning to secular occupations. Some remain in their "paying" jobs after

TABLE 22
Career Attainment

POSITION	% Goal Ever		% Actual Full-time Placements	
	Male	Female	Male	Female
Church Administrator	10%	12%	13%	6%
Director of Christian Education	37	63	2	4
Military Chaplain	10	4	5	.9
Global Missionary	4	5	.6	.6
Pastor	63	37	49	21
Assistant Pastor	6	11	14	12
Church Ministry Founder	12	20	5	6
Evangelist	8	15	3	.6
Guest Speaker	13	22	12	11
Consultant	10	14	5	4
Counselor	17	24	7	7
Youth Minister	8	7	4	1

seminary. The only explanation for this is their call to ministry is a true calling, regardless of the cost or the earthly reward.

When comparing the career goals to actual full-time placements, the women hit the mark with regard to some positions. In other words, the percentage of those who aspired to that position was nearly the same as the percentage who have worked in that position since seminary. The women's aspirations were equal to the placements as assistant pastor (12 percent). On the other hand, the clergymen in the sample filled assistant pastor positions more frequently than they had aspired to them (6 percent goal, 14 percent placements). More women wanted to be pastors than were pastors (37 percent goal, 21 percent placement). This was also true of almost every position reported. Director of Christian education (63 percent goal, 4 percent placement) exhibited the most overwhelming contrast between career goals and positionality. Consultant and counselor are similarly undersubscribed. These may be good part-time options, but they are not the bread and butter of the profession.

The career goals do not match actual opportunities. Perhaps this reveals some dissatisfaction with the pay, the working conditions, or the status associated with pastoring in an environment where so many successful pastors do not have a seminary education.

Mentors and Role Models

Seventy-five percent of the women respondents have had primarily male mentors. Although the majority of mentors have been male, the women expressed a great need for female role models as documented in *The Irresistible Urge to Preach* (Meyers). Although women had been mentored by male leaders, it was not until they had seen a woman preaching or presiding in the pulpit that they achieved greater comfort with their own call to ministry.

The gender of mentors is similar to the discussion of mentors in chapter 5. There is one exception. While the second mentor shows an increase in the percent of female mentors for both men and women, the third mentor reverts to a higher male mentorship of men and women.

TABLE 23
Mentors by Gender

	MENTOR 1		MENTOR 2		MENTOR 3	
	Male	Female	Male	Female	Male	Female
Male Clergy	92%	7%	68%	32%	73%	27%
Female Clergy	67%	33%	56%	44%	58%	42%

Looking at Mentor 1, 7 percent of the men had women mentors and 33 percent of the females had same-sex mentors. It is noteworthy that as men and women list a second mentor, female mentors increased to 32 percent for men and 44 percent for female). A more dramatic increase is observed in men. While first-listed mentors were only 7 percent female, second-listed were 32 percent female.

When asked to give the relationship that they had with their mentors, the following answers were given:

Overwhelmingly, the pastor was the most frequent mentor of these women. After pastor came other clergy, friends, and professors.

TABLE 24
Mentoring Relationships

	Mentor 1	Mentor 2	Mentor 3
Pastor	40%	24%	4%
Friend	19%	18%	25%
Other Clergy	13%	14%	18%
Relatives	7%	8%	10%
Professor	8%	15%	16%
Other	13%	21%	27%

The females who mentored females were 20 percent friends, 17 percent clergy, 13 percent professors, and 35 percent other, including counselor, deacon, elder, employee, laywoman, mother, other relatives, prayer partner, student, and supervisor. By contrast, men who mentored other men were 37 percent pastors, 21 percent friends, 14 percent professors, 12 percent other clergy, and 16 percent other. Men are being mentored to a greater extent by pastors. Friends and professors equally mentor same-sex mentees for both men and women at 20–21 percent for friends and 13–14 percent for professors. The major differences are that men are more likely to be mentored by male pastors. Women are more likely to be mentored by women ministers who are not pastors.

Practice of Ministry

Ministry is multitasked. From among a list of ministerial functions, each respondent selected three tasks in each of the categories discussed below. The women indicated that people are helped the most through teaching, preaching, and counseling. When asked what three activities they enjoyed most, 76 percent indicated teaching, 66 percent preaching, and 34 percent counseling. The practices they enjoyed least were fund-raising (69 percent), civic and political leadership (45 percent), and administration (31 percent).

Table 25 (p. 161) shows the areas of ministry viewed as most helpful, enjoyed the most, and least enjoyed.

In 1999 the clergywomen designated preaching (68 percent) and teaching (72 percent) as the practices of ministry that were most helpful to people. Counseling was rated as most helpful by 51 percent, with visitation at a distant 24 percent. Social service, administration, and fellowship followed at 12 percent, 11 percent, and 11 percent, respectively.

Preaching and teaching ranked at 66 percent and 76 percent, respectively, among practices that the women ministers enjoyed most. Counseling was ranked at 31 percent. Among those practices enjoyed least by these ministers are fund-raising, civic and political leadership, administration, prophecy, visitation, and community organization.

TABLE 25
Most Helpful Areas of Ministry

Area of Ministry	1992 Valid %	1999 Valid %
Preaching	68	68
Teaching	65	72
Visitation	26	25
Administration	14	11
Social Services	11	12
Fellowship	14	11
Counseling	55	51
Laying on Hands	12	11

Areas of Ministry Enjoyed Most

Area of Ministry	1992 Valid %	1999 Valid %
Preaching	67	66
Teaching	71	76
Singing	16	11
Counseling	44	34
Visitation	21	21
Fellowship	18	10
Administration	11	12
Social Service	12	13

Areas of Ministry Enjoyed Least

Area of Ministry	1992 Valid %	1999 Valid %
Evangelist	11	5
Playing Instruments	11	25
Visitation	14	9
Administration	30	31
Stewardship	12	8
Fund-raising	54	69
Community Organization	12	10
Civic & Political Leadership	27	45

There are differences in what these black men and women view as the most satisfying aspects of ministry. In the areas of ministry that help people the most, the men (81 percent) ranked preaching more often than did women (68 percent). On the other hand, women (51 percent) ranked counseling higher than did the men (44 percent). With regard to preaching, it has greater favor among men, who have such famous role models as Rev. Martin Luther King, Jr., Rev. C. L. Franklin, and today, Bishop T. D. Jakes. *Ebony* magazine has periodically honored the fifteen greatest African American preachers. Contemporary giants include Rev. Garner Taylor, Rev. James Forbes, and Rev. H. Beecher Hicks. Only recently have women been included on this list.

It is interesting that visitation ranked at 23 percent for men and 25 percent for women—roughly one-fourth. This seems low, since it is generally believed that congregants highly value visitation, especially during times of serious illness and bereavement. One often hears chronic complaints among parishioners that certain members have not been visited by the minister. It is commonly held that ministers do not have time for such visitations, given the many demands upon them and the multifaceted dimensions of their occupations. However, this finding indicates that two-thirds of them did not rank visitation in the top three most helpful activities.

There was substantial difference between men and women in how they viewed laying-on-of-hands. Only 3 percent of men included it in the three most helpful activities. Twelve percent of women chose it. Since nineteenth-century African American female religious leaders laid a rich foundation in preaching, singing, and evangelism, it persists among black clergywomen, praying grandmothers, and church mothers. In fact, this practice among black females was sometimes necessitated by the lack of medical care available to children of slaves and sharecroppers. When medical doctors and hospitals were inaccessible, family members would ask spiritual women to pray. The author's grandmother was such a praying woman. She was one of those African women who would rub you as she prayed for you or talked to you. Hands such as hers became known as "healing hands." Therefore, laying-on-of-hands points to both the biblical spiritual gift of healing (Romans, 1 Corinthians, James) and the cultural invention of necessity, that is, since medical care was not available, black women orchestrated the healing power of prayer through human touch. Men were well known to take people's hands and pray; but in more desperate situations, some black women were known to carry anointed, perfumed olive oil with them and bring it out and use it as they laid hands on various parts of the body, especially the head. Psalm 23 says, "You [God] anoint my head with oil." Even today African American clergywomen do not experience any embarrassment in following the example of Jesus in this regard, believing that God will work through them as God did through the early apostles.

Similarly, black women have a long, successful track record as teachers and feel very comfortable in this modality. The degree of helpfulness of counseling exceeded its level of enjoyment. This indicates that these ministers recognize that it is more helpful than it is enjoyed. This is because of the three factors of skill, stress, and time. Counseling is extremely time-consuming in a one-on-one practice. Preaching and teaching allow the minister to reach larger numbers of persons at one time. Because ministers spend so much time assisting people in crisis, the counseling component is stressful. Ministers are often overwhelmed by the burdens and problems of others as they try to comfort them or spiritually advise them. It is good to refer persons to professionals, but the fear is that they are not willing to pay the required fees. It would be helpful if more laypeople who are specially trained in counseling would make their services available at reduced rates. Most ministers want more training in the counseling and biblical studies area. The church offers spiritual therapy and needs the full complement of emotional and psychological astuteness that can help parishioners deal with relationship problems, conflict, addictions, and mental illness. The team ministry will be most helpful in addressing this need. There are ordained women who wish to specialize in the counseling area who can be more fully utilized to meet this need after extensive training.

Another striking difference between men and women is in the enjoyment of fellowship. It ranks as one of the three most enjoyed for 15 percent of men and 10 percent of women. This finding parallels the finding that the ministry has helped the social lives of men (24 percent) more than those of women (18 percent).

What practices are liked the least among these ministries? Fundraising ranked highly at 63 percent, civic/political leadership at 41 percent, and administration weighed in at 32 percent. It may be that these are areas that ministers should delegate to laity. But unless a trusted ally does administration, another church leader can undermine, stall, and sabotage programmatic, facility- and finance-related activities that forward the vision of the pastor. Loyal pastoral assistants can be helpful, but if they are ordained and do not enjoy these duties any more than the pastor does, there will be a turnover as they move out of these leadership roles into ones more closely resembling the pastor's. Trusted family members and/or quasi-family member types seem to work best in such positions. Corporately and professionally trained laity have much to offer the church. But someone has to train them in the unique mission, climate, and politics of a particular congregation's life.

Social Practices

On a scale of one to ten, the women were asked to register their approval or disapproval of certain controversial social practices. The items in Table 26 include changing ecclesiastical language in light of the women's movement, that is, using inclusive language and referring to God as "Mother" or "She." The other items represent behaviors that some church leaders and ministers have debated as negative over the past decade. They might be called modern-day sins, which weaken the moral fiber of society and are in violation of biblical teachings. The responses recorded as one to five were counted as an approval. Items recorded as six to ten were counted as a disapproval. Simple percentages of the women who approved of each social practice are recorded below. The 1992 approval rating of 203 clergywomen is also listed for comparison purposes.

The feminist/womanist developments over the past twenty years have led black women to embrace the changing language that is inclusive of women. This new language replaces the older, so-called generic male-dominated language. Seventy-five percent of the respondents approve of this development. To a lesser degree (55 percent), they also approve of female imaging of God, for example, "Mother" and "She." In the early seventies when many white feminists were writing about the new language agenda, it was not clear to what extent black women would embrace this agenda. It is clear from this survey that it has had an important impact on black religious women.

It is interesting to note that there is a movement toward a more conservative stance on all of the issues presented. Those with at least a 10 percent drop in approval include: divorce, adjustment of

TABLE 26
Social Issues

Area of Ministry	1999 Approval Rate	1992 Approval Rate
Inclusive Language	75%	83%
Calling God "Mother" or "She"	55%	61%
Divorce	47%	59%
Adjustment of Church to Science	34%	46%
Surrogate Mothering	30%	32%
Ordination of Homosexuals	25%	31%
Abortion	23%	37%
Homosexual Adoption of Children	23%	32%
Alcohol Consumption	20%	26%
Homosexual Marriage	17%	22%
Euthanasia	16%	31%
Legalized Gambling	13%	23%
Bisexuality	11%	9%
Premarital Sex	10%	27%
Smoking Tobacco	9%	13%
Adultery	5%	11%
Pornography	7%	6%

church to science, abortion, euthanasia, legalized gambling, and premarital sex. The lowering of approval may be due to the larger number of Southern Baptists in the sample. It is also true that American religion seems to be tilting toward a more conservative posture. The evangelical, conservative wing of Christianity has made a tremendous gain in publishing and television broadcasting. The media influence may have a strong effect upon the average church-goer. American religion has entered a post-liberal era.

Spirituality: Images of God

Theology consists of having God on our minds. From among twenty-three choices presented, participants were asked to select all the God images appropriate. There are two ways of considering the images that these women have in mind when they think about God. The first is to look at those images that 90 percent or more of the clergywomen checked as thinking of God "much of the time" in 1999. The second is to combine the "much of the time" and the "some of the time" responses. For the latter, both 1999 and 1992 results are given.

There is little change in the images that are most important to these women. In 1985, 120 black clergywomen wrote Creator as their most frequent image of God. Creator still holds the number one spot throughout 1992 and 1999. Help has climbed upward slightly by 2 percent. Liberator has also gained almost 3 percent and friend almost 2 percent. Father, Son, and Holy Spirit dropped by 5 percent. Father gained almost 9 percent. This is a significant finding in the face of inclusive language that tries to move away

TABLE 27
Images of God

	Much of the Time 1999	Much & Some of the Time	
	1999	1999	1992
Creator	98%	100%	99%
Healer	95%	99.7%	99.5%
Protector	94%	99.3%	98.5%
Spirit	94%	99.7%	99.5%
Help	94%	99.7%	97.5%
Wisdom	92%	99.3%	98.5%
Liberator	91%	99.0%	96.1%
Friend	90%	99.4%	97.5%
Father, Son, Holy Spirit		99%	93.6%
Father		96.4%	87.7%
Mystery		96.3%	94.1%
Jesus		95.8%	94.6%
Encompassing Presence		95.6%	92.6%
Master		94.3%	86.2%
Judge		90.0%	88.2%

from exclusively male language. In spite of this trend, the image of God the Father, though not highly rated in the "much of the time" category, has kept and gained strength in the "some of the time" category. One reason Father retains its power is that it was the favorite image of Jesus, who often referred to God as Father and taught his disciples to do the same as evidenced in the Lord's Prayer, which begins, "Our Father." All of the remaining "some of the time" additions gained more strength in 1999. Mystery, Jesus, Encompassing Presence, Master, and Judge seem to have a permanent place in these women's arsenals of faith. Master saw the greatest increase with an additional 8 percent. This is the title that the disciples often used when referring to Jesus.

Restricting their choice to only one image, the women indicated that the single most important or pivotal God image was Father, Son, and Holy Spirit (28 percent), Spirit (13 percent), Father (10 percent), and Liberator (10 percent). There is no doubt that the trinitarian formula incorporates several strong images, including Father and Spirit. These two are named in singular form with the addition of Liberator. The fact that the largest single score was 28 percent demonstrates that people think of God according to their need at that time. God remains the I Am of every need.

A listing of the respondents' "much of the time" images of God were checked with the following frequency: Creator was checked by 92 percent; Spirit by 90 percent; Liberator, Healer, Protector, and Help by 87 percent; Wisdom by 85 percent; and Friend by 84 percent. Images selected "much" and "some" of the time combined identified additional images that ranked among the most frequently chosen. They were Father (97 percent), Jesus (97 percent), and Encompassing Presence (95 percent). Those images that received the highest percentages of "none of the time" were Goddess (65 percent), Mother (25 percent), Creator-Destroyer (21 percent), Lover (19 percent), and Elementary Force in Nature (18 percent).

Twenty-three images of God were listed. Men and women were asked to check whether they used each image to envision God much of the time, some of the time, or none of the time. Therefore, the percentage of persons who checked each image established the extent to which this sample saw God in that image.

Comparing male and female choices from among the twenty-three images presented, there was a striking similarity between the male and female selections. This was most clearly seen when they were asked to choose only one image as most important or pivotal in their perception of God. The four God images receiving the most checks were the same for men and women but selected in a slightly different order.

When respondents were asked to pick one pivotal image of God, the images listed in Table 28 received the highest number of votes by gender.

TABLE 28
Most Pivotal Images of God

Males		Females	
Father, Son, Holy Spirit	28%	Father, Son, Holy Spirit	26%
Father	16%	Spirit	13%
Spirit	8%	Liberator	9%
Liberator	8%	Father	9%

Both men and women chose the trinitarian formula most often. Please note that the Trinity includes both Father and Spirit, which are also on the list in solo form. The one addition to the list is Liberator.

Perceptions about Women in Ministry

Before moving to a discussion of specific promoters and inhibitors of black women's gaining greater acceptance and opportunity in ministry, it is helpful to start with general perceptions about black women in ministry. The issue of women in the ministry remains a burning one throughout the black church. Evidence of the problems and the need for change is reflected in the perceptions that men and women expressed in the survey.

Starting with the women themselves, at least 60 percent agreed with the following statements: There should be more women in executive staff positions in regional and national offices within their denominations. More women should be ordained to full ordination status. There should be more hymns and prayers using female imagery and names for God. More women in the clergy do not lower the prestige of the ordained ministry. If women take over more of the leadership roles in the church, men's participation will not drop further. Women do not have as easy a time as men in becoming ordained to full-clergy status. Women, whether lay or clergy, do not hold positions of influence in their region comparable to laymen and clergymen. Women do not have as easy a time as men do in becoming senior pastors in congregations. Women over fifty have a more difficult time than men getting any full-time ministry positions.

Are there differences in the ways that black male and female clergy feel about women in the ministry? If so, how wide are those disparities? Not surprisingly, women respondents were more sympathetic to denominational changes favoring the leadership of women. The 476 men who completed the questionnaire acknowledged in numerous ways the larger challenges that women in ministry face.

Only 56 percent of the men agreed that there should be more women in executive staff positions in regional and national offices of their denominations. Eighty-one percent of the women agreed. In this case, respondents from the three black Methodist denominations (A.M.E., A.M.E.Z., and C.M.E.) and the American Baptist denominations held a higher level of agreement. The Black Methodists dominate here. Until recently, none of them had elected a woman bishop. The A.M.E. church was the first to break the "stained-glass ceiling" by appointing Rev. Vashti McKenzie to serve as bishop in 2000. Of course, there have been other black denominations that have consecrated African American female bishops. Such churches included Mount Sinai Holy Church of America, which was founded by Bishop Ida B. Robinson, and whose presiding prelate has always been a woman, and Mount Calvary Holy Church of America, which also consecrated its first black woman bishop several years ago. The A.M.E. church is very important, however, because it is considered the oldest black denomination in the United States, and it is recognized as one of the seven historic black denominations represented within the Congress of National Black Churches.

With regard to recent progress, more men than women thought that ordained women were more accepted in 1999 than they were five years ago (71 percent male, 54 percent female). Again, the men and women showed some degree of disparity with regard to the current status of women in the church. When asked if women held positions of influence in their region, 47 percent of men and 63 percent of women disagreed. One might conclude at this point that the men were more optimistic about the plight of clergywomen than were the women themselves.

The preference for inclusive language is one measure of feminism, according to Zikmund, Lummis, and Chang. When asked whether or not they found inclusive language during scripture reading disruptive, 52 percent of men and 67 percent of women said no. Those who said yes included 21 percent of the men and only 10 percent of the women. Approximately one-fourth of both groups acknowledged that they had mixed feelings on this issue (28 percent men, 23 percent women). Should there be more hymns with female imagery? Approximately one-third of the women (33 percent) said yes and almost a third (31 percent) said no. Turning to the male responses on the same question, 18 percent said yes and 51 percent said no. Both black male and female clergy seemed to be more positive toward inclusive language during scripture reading than they were toward changing the hymns or their lyrics. Changing hymn lyrics would be more difficult than changing the biblical text. The newer translations of the Bible have opened persons to varying the language used in scripture reading. The *New Revised Standard Version Bible* has changed the exclusively male language wherever the original biblical language allowed.

The support of the clergy brothers in this survey is commendable. When asked to comment on the statement "Clergymen are threatened by clergywomen," 25 percent of men agreed, 39 percent disagreed, and 37 percent had mixed feelings. The women supported the sentiment, with only 10 percent disagreeing. More than half of the women (59 percent) agreed, and 37 percent registered mixed feelings, the same level as the men. In this case women were more convinced than men that clergymen were indeed threatened by clergywomen. These findings attest to the hurdles that women ministers face in the contemporary black church.

Promoters of Ministerial Opportunity

By design, the women were asked to identify the factors that they felt promoted the greater acceptance of themselves as ministers and would increase their ministerial opportunities. Promoters of ministerial opportunity were identified, first for 1992 and then for 1999.

TABLE 29
Promoters According to Black Clergywomen

	Promoters	1992	1999
1	Completion of Seminary	87%	80%
2	Spiritual Maturity	78%	75%
3	Leadership Ability	78%	57%
4	Personal Qualities	71%	56%
5	Clergywomen	69%	34%
6	Interpersonal Skills	70%	51%
7	Family Support	69%	50%
8	Oratorical Skills	68%	45%

What promotes wider acceptance and greater opportunity for women ministers? These women have identified some very specific things. What is striking is that women are not looking to men to do it for them. Nor are they focusing upon the great "isms," which are beyond their control. They are focusing on things that they can do. This demonstrates a realization of their emphasis upon self-reliance.

Between 1992 and 1999 there has been a shift with regard to some of the strong promoters. The most obvious is other women ministers. While it was considered important to 69 percent in the 1992 sample, it was only checked by 34 percent in 1999. This parallels the finding in 1999 that female clergy are inhibitors, according to 47 percent. This is an increase over the 31 percent that checked female clergy as an inhibitor in 1992. Perhaps the emergence of more and more black clergywomen has not led to women ministers' helping other women ministers as much as was expected. There may be a need to structure more mentoring opportunities for women with women. This would probably be better done across denominational lines. Currently, most of the women who are in support groups are in mixed-gender groups. Again, there may be the phenomenon of the oppressed becoming the oppressor. In seminary classes, women testify to poor experiences with women ministers. This oppression may be experienced because women are so new to the profession that once they are in positions, they are reluctant to elevate and promote other women ministers. It is often stated, "Where did all of these women come from?" One laywoman stated that seeing so many women in the pulpit is "unnatural." In the past, women's collectives have been a source of empowerment to women in all professions, including the ministry. Perhaps the female majority in the membership of the black church plants a fear of feminization of the church when too many women cluster in leadership. In addition, because women ministers may feel vulnerable and fragile in their status in the church and not as secure as men, they may have difficulty reaching out to promote other women.

Among the personal attributes that are holding their own across both years are seminary education, spiritual maturity, and leadership skills. Losing ground as promoters are family support and oratorical skills. The latter is encouraging, because the image of the black minister as a hard, fervent preacher who is a master orator like Martin Luther King, Jr., has kept the more soft-spoken females from the ministry. Today there are a variety of styles being affirmed among women, which makes room for a leadership group that is more diverse both in sermon delivery and personality. This will put the ministry on a more professional footing, thus making it more accessible to women as a whole.

Inhibitors of Ministerial Opportunity

Inhibitors of ministerial opportunity checked most often are listed in Table 30, first for 1992 and then for 1999.

TABLE 30
Inhibitors According to Black Clergywomen

	Inhibitors	1992	1999
1	Sexism	94%	90%
2	Male Clergy	81%	61%
3	Racism	71%	52%
4	Female Laity	67%	20%
5	Female Clergy	31%	47%
6	Lack of Leadership Skills	56%	42%
7	Weak Interpersonal Skills	53%	13%
8	Lack of Mentors	53%	9%
9	Male Laity	47%	18%
10	Weak Oratorical Skills	46%	10%
11	Lack of Advocacy	41%	36%
12	Lack of Family Support	42%	40%
13	Physical Appearance	28%	29%
14	Lack of Seminary	54%	12%
15	Divorced Status	20%	40%

The good news here is that the level of intensity registered for each inhibitor has decreased in every case, except female clergy and divorced status. The former has been discussed above. Divorce does not register as a strong inhibitor, but as more of an inhibitor in 1999 than in 1992. It went from a 20 percent mention to a 40 percent mention. It is something that warrants attention in future research. It can be speculated that the new emphasis on restoring family values may account for its added strength in 1999. Also, the fact that more conservative denominations, for example, Southern Baptists, are represented in this sample may explain its higher rating as an inhibitor.

Four of the inhibitors presented here are gender-related: sexism, male clergy, female laity, and male laity. Sexism and male clergy were listed as the top two inhibitors in the 1985, 1992, and 1999 studies. Sexism relates to institutional and historical factors that have led to discrimination against the equal treatment of women in the ministry. The item male clergy refers to the lack of support among male colleagues. This is disappointing, since male clergy are perceived as the power brokers of the American religious establishment.

Fourth on the list of inhibitors is female laity. In this area, there is a change for the better. The closer alignment of female clergy and laity appears to have taken place within the seven-year interval. Female laity as an inhibitor declined from 67 percent mentioning them in 1992 to only 20 percent mentioning them in 1999. This is cause for great celebration and may be the greatest single sign of increased hopefulness in the 1999 study. With greater focus on the need to employ more black clergywomen in paid positions within the church, female laity can be significant allies in helping clergywomen attain this goal.

Weak interpersonal skills are also greatly improved. Its damage to ministerial opportunity has dropped from 53 percent of the women mentioning it to only 13 percent mentioning it. The climate may be more affirming of the personality traits of black women ministers. In the earlier decades, there was a stereotype of these women ministers being bitter due to the negative experiences that they had encountered. Perhaps as acceptance is growing, fewer women ministers are labeled "troublemakers," a disenchanted, bitter presence in ecclesiastical circles. Another positive sign is that more mentors seem to be available to sponsor these women. Consequently, the lack of mentors fell drastically from 53 percent checking it as an inhibitor in 1992 to a mere 9 percent in 1999.

Finally, and a bit more disheartening, is the lower importance placed on the lack of seminary. It seems a paradox that seminary education, which is a promoter of high proportion, does not produce a similar negative effect as an inhibitor when it is absent. What may be happening here is that these women are aware that many churches will call a nonseminary-trained minister before calling a learned clergywoman to fill a salaried position on the ministerial staff, most especially as pastor. It seems that institutions of graduate theological education and denominations alike should be concerned about this and seek ways to improve the placement of women who have completed seminary. Great progress has been made in the last thirty years regarding blacks receiving M.Div. degrees. This credentialling has been put in place in most white, mainline churches. It has been less important in black denominations. For example, the A.M.E. church in some regions of the country requires only the bachelor's degree. Another factor in the hiring of pastors is the tendency for black churches to reach outside their own denominations to get a pastor, more so in congregational polity groups, which are called "free" churches, than in the episcopal groups, where bishops and district overseers appoint persons within their own denominations. One of the predominately white denominations has received money to recruit more African American ministers to offset the large number of retirements anticipated in the near future. When the pool of seminary graduates was reviewed, two-thirds were female, where-upon one of the prominent elders of this church declared, "We must do something to prepare our churches to receive these women as pastors." Fearing that women pastors may have an adverse effect upon the growth of the church, congregations are not willing to risk hiring a woman pastor. Therefore, intentional education and consciousness-raising are necessary as an interval. When asked if their search committees would consider a woman as pastor, repeatedly larger churches give a resounding, "No, I don't think so." One denomination has decided to produce a study guide to assist with this problem. In one region of this denomination, positive letters about women pastors were compiled and published in booklet form. More of such intentional advocacy efforts are needed.

Ministerial Opportunity

In the 1999 study, men and women were asked what they think inhibits the acceptance of and opportunity for women ministers. The following were their responses.

The total highest-ranking responses are: (1) sexism, (2) male clergy, (3) racism, and (4) female clergy. Also highly ranked are lack of leadership ability, lack of family, lack of advocacy, and divorced status. Divorced status is perceived as three times more damaging than being unmarried, which received only 11 percent support. Very interesting is the much higher inhibition on the part of the clergy over the laity. The response of male clergy (57 percent) looms over female clergy (41 percent) because male clergy still have the most power. This reflects the fact that it is the clergy and not the laity who are the gatekeepers of ordination, placement, and promotion within the ministry. This is the nature of the ministerial profession, in that

Table 31
Inhibitors of Clergywomen by Gender

Inhibitors	Male	Female	Total
Sexism	76%	90%	82%
Racism	45%	51%	48%
Male Clergy	55%	61%	57%
Male Laity	9%	18%	12%
Female Clergy	35%	49%	41%
Female Laity	29%	20%	25%
Lack of Family	30%	41%	34%
Womanism	13%	24%	19%
Lack of Advocacy	31%	37%	33%
Physical Appearance	28%	30%	28%
Anointing with Oil	15%	2%	10%
Biblical Passages	12%	14%	13%
Divorced Status	32%	39%	35%
Unmarried Status	12%	10%	11%
Lack of Leadership Ability	33%	43%	37%
Lack of Mentor/Sponsor	8%	9%	9%

it is peer evaluated. Turning to the topic of male and female laity, both men and women agree that the greater hurdles are placed there by female laity rather than by male laity, two to one. Clergymen ranked male laity at 9 percent, much lower than the rating of clergywomen at 18 percent. Apparently, clergymen do not get many complaints from laymen about clergymen. This data indicates that they get three times more complaints from laywomen. This finding corresponds to the familiar comment on the part of clergymen to the effect that women are more opposed to women ministers than are men. Of course, they are not factoring in themselves as more significant inhibitors. Sexism as an inhibitor to ministerial opportunity towers head and shoulders above all else. Although women think this more than do men (90 percent to 76 percent), three quarters of men and almost all the women are in agreement that sexism is alive and well in the black church.

Based upon this data, several observations are curious and need further investigation. For example, why would more women than men consider womanism an inhibitor (24 percent to 13 percent)? It is surprising that physical appearance is so powerful. Other leadership studies need to be done to explain its appeal. The anointing with oil deliverance ministry is the final major difference between male and female responses. Only 2 percent of women considered it an inhibitor, compared to 12 percent of the men. Women are viewing the retention of this earlier priestly tradition as a healthy part of ministry. It blends well with the growing neo-Pentecostal nature of the black church as discussed in Lincoln and Mamiya's *The Black Church in the African American Experience.* Faith-healing ministries continue, especially through the television ministries of modern-day charismatic churches.

It is surprising that biblical injunctions are rated so low when one often hears the Corinthians "Women should be silent in the churches" (1 Cor. 14:34) and the Timothy "I permit no woman to teach" (1 Tim. 2:12) passages hurled as definitive proclamations of prohibition against women preachers and pastors. Its total 13 percent suggests that the clergy themselves interpret scripture as not opposing women in ministry. The biblical texts that are used against women are historically based and address particular problems within particular churches; they were never intended to be used to silence women in every church for all time. In the case of the Timothy passage, the issue is not that women should not teach, but rather that unlearned women who are teaching heresy should not teach. In Acts, Priscilla and her husband are commended for *their* correct teaching of Apollos, and in Romans *they* are placed over large numbers of churches. Any ground that was lost for women by Eve in the garden has been more than regained through Jesus Christ, whose mother, Mary, brought forth the Word of God incarnate. Christian women are no longer living under the curse of Genesis. According to New Testament scripture, Christ has set all women free, as demonstrated particularly in the liberation of the woman caught in adultery, the woman with the issue of blood, the Samaritan woman, the Syro-Phoenician woman, and the woman bent over.

As shown above, there is great similarity between the answers of males and females regarding ministerial inhibitors. Except for the responses of female laity, lack of seminary, and anointing with oil, a higher proportion of women than men believe that each of the items listed are inhibitors to the acceptance and promotion of female clergy. Sexism ranked first by both with 90 percent of the women acknowledging it. The one factor rated more highly by women than by men is female clergy. It is not clear what this means. However, one may speculate that higher expectations and negative personal experience with female clergy can account for it. Perhaps a lower percentage of men have worked with female clergy. On the other hand, more men checked female laity than women. More men seem to believe that the opposition of women in the church by women preachers is widespread. It has been the author's experience that the largest number of active supporters of her ministry have been women. In spite of this, those men who actively supported the ministry were very outspoken about the reality of sexism.

Conclusion

How do women advance as professionals within the clergy? In the face of sexism, there are clearly a few important factors that enhance the advancement of clergywomen. Among these are hard work and an understanding that the scriptures, which on the surface appear prohibitive, were written to particular situations and were not intended for universal application against all women for all time, everywhere. Another promoter is the acquisition of higher levels of education that elucidate these truths and better prepare ministers to serve God's people. There must be affirmative action–type programs to open doors for qualified female ministers. And there must be time to deprogram what people have systematically been taught that was not altogether correct, yet was believed to be sacred.

To pursue a professional career in any field, one needs to know how many jobs are available to her or him. It is clear that most of the positions available in the profession are in pastorate and assistant pastorate positions. In this sample of 324 clergywomen, sixty-nine have been paid full-time pastors and thirty-two have been paid part-time pastors. This is a combined total of 101 women pastors. Thirty-nine have been paid full-time assistant pastors and sixty-two have been paid part-time assistant pastors. This is a combined total of 101 women assistant pastors. Together they make up an opportunity structure of 202 positions.

In 1985 only 11 percent of the 120 women had been full-time pastors. In 1992, 36 percent had been full-time pastors. While there had been an increase in the percentage of women who had pastored in the first two studies, there was a decline in 1999. Numerically, the numbers of full-time women pastors rose from thirteen in 1985 to seventy-three in 1992; it declined to sixty-nine in 1999. This shows that there must be a more concerted effort of advocacy to produce a positive, more progressive advancement of black clergywomen. The decline is still much smaller than the previous increase.

Another important factor is salary. Overall, the salaries for ministry-related jobs are quite low for men and women. However, they are even lower for women. While the mean for men falls within the $30,000 range, the mean for women falls within the $20,000 range. This is a salary gap of $10,000. This is especially limiting for 71 percent of the women in the study who have to support children.

Black women often say, "I think I could be an assistant, but I don't want to be a pastor." Speculation is that some of the women who say this are fearful of rejection, are lacking same-sex mentoring, or perhaps are fearful of success itself. Some are entrenched in the so-called "sacred" traditional teachings of men being the heads of the church and the family, and of God being anthropomorphic in the role of Father.

While much has been written about social change, not much has been written about social change within African American religious institutions. The needed change spoken of is gender. For this change to take place it has to be undergirded by two important pillars—one is the acceptance of the historical-critical method of biblical interpretation, and the other is womanist theology. One deals with the sacred texts that are the authoritative foundations of the community. The other deals with how people think about God-ordained systems, in this case, the church. What people have been taught and are learning shapes the structure and content of their beliefs and self-actualization. According to the newspaper the *Virginian-Pilot* (June 2000), at a conference of more than 5,600 African American clergy, women ministers defended their right to serve the church as pastors. Bishop Barbara Amos, founder of Faith Deliverance Christian Center in Norfolk, Virginia, said, "We all know that evil thrives in institutions. But anything systematically taught in us has to be systematically taught out of us."

There is another countervailing authority within the black religious community. It is Spirit—the animating connection in the divine-human encounter. The Spirit has been well-established as being neither male nor female. It is transgendered and cannot be contained by human categorization. It is this authority that has rooted and grounded the calling and anointing of black women for ministry. It has been personal and corporate in its manifestation, but how it intersects with ecclesiastical life is of great interest to the subject at hand. It appears that the leveraging points for change were first the scholarly interpretation of the scriptures and womanist theology.

Both of these are firmly established within the curriculum of graduate theological education.

Another movement in this progression toward social change was how to empower black people to transcend the social-psychological obstacles to the full acceptance and enhancement of African American clergywomen. This may be called "transgender freedom within a religious liberation movement." First was Spirit and the black woman's call to preach. Second was the historical-critical method of interpreting the Bible that threw off the bondage of restrictive texts against women. Third was the formulation of womanist theology within the reconstruction of liberationist theologies. The fourth will be the social-psychological freedom of black men and women to remove gender as a defining factor in institutional leadership. As the fourth step is being accomplished, talented, well-equipped, and well-trained women will overcome their hesitancy to move forward as a professional group. In this process, larger numbers of women will view assistant pastor as a step toward the pastorate. This will propel a growing number of laywomen into other leadership positions in the church that have traditionally been filled by men, for example, financial officers, property officers, deacons, and trustees. At that point, gender shift as a contemporary social change within the church will be complete. Happily, it has already begun.

Black women are rooted and grounded in preaching the gospel and providing leadership in the church. The latter decades of the twentieth century have brought progress in the status of black women clergy. Their resilience and strength in the face of many challenges leads one to embrace the notion that they will continue to persevere at whatever level possible. As the United States of America enters a new millennium, black clergywomen are well aware of the new heights and depths available to them through Christ Jesus. An increasing number of them are God-led to set their sights in new directions and to aim their arrows high. Even if they fail to hit the mark, they will know that they have done their part to move the kingdom of God forward.

Black women are touching many lives with the life-giving message of the gospel of Jesus Christ. This is their hour of opportunity. This is the time to give them honor. Many unnamed biblical women up to now have received little or no recognition. Now they should be remembered and honored. God has already honored them to carry his word and to exalt his Son. Regarding contemporary women, no longer will a token few circumscribe their opportunity. They are walking into arenas that are new and foreign to them every day. They are graciously taking their places at the table of recognized influence. More and more the whole world wants to hear what black women ministers have to say. The whole world is receiving the hope that they dispense. The world wants their care and touch. Their service can no longer go unrecognized. It is a time for honor. In the Holy Scriptures glory and honor go together. As the glory of God is revealed to be upon them, the elevation of honor must be bestowed. It is refreshing to discover that there is new revelation from God to this generation. Minister Louis Farrakhan called for the elevation of women into the Christian pulpit and out of the clutches of sexism. Many women of all faiths rose to their feet at his Million Family March, which was held at the steps of the nation's capital on October 16, 2000. The next week, former president Jimmy Carter held a news conference that went across national television. He announced that his 155-year-old Southern Baptist congregation was withdrawing from the Southern Baptist Conference because of its mandate to refuse the ordination of women pastors. Honor is not just a feeling of respect, but an outward expression of that feeling. Because of the faithfulness and fruitfulness of clergywomen, it is time for honor— honor by way of equal pay, equal placement, and equal opportunity. For African American clergywomen, the ultimate honor comes whenever they can use their gifts and graces to the fullest and in the service of God's people. In this way they honor their Creator. To not maximize their potential is to dishonor God, who gives purpose, meaning, and destiny to everyone. Giving increased honor to women is not an end unto itself, for as women of honor advance, they reflect God's glory. This is the greater end.

References

Andrews, William L. *Sisters of the Spirit*. Bloomington, Ind.: Indiana University Press, 1986.

Bacote, Samuel William. *Who's Who Among the Colored Baptists in the United States*. Kansas City, Kan.: Franklin Hudson, 1913.

Barfoot, Charles H., and Gerald T. Sheppard. "Prophetic vs. Priestly Religion: The Changing Role of Women Clergy in Pentecostal Churches." *Review of Religious Research* 22 (1980): 2–17.

Barnett, H. G. *Innovation: The Basis of Cultural Change*. New York: McGraw-Hill, 1953.

Becker, Howard S., et al. *Boys in White: Student Culture in Medical School*. Chicago: University of Chicago Press, 1961.

Berger, Peter, et al. *The Homeless Mind*. New York: Random House, 1973.

Blassingame, John. *Slave Testimony*. Baton Rouge: Louisiana State University Press, 1977.

Bourne, P. G., and N. J. Wikler. "Commitment and the Cultural Mandate: Women in Medicine." *Social Problems* 25 (1978): 430–40.

Bradley, David H. *A History of the African Methodist Episcopal Zion Church*. Nashville: Parthenon Press, 1956.

Brock, Rita N., Claudia Camp, Serene Jones. *Setting the Table: Women in Theological Conversation*. St. Louis: Chalice Press, 1995.

Brooks, Evelyn. *The Women's Movement in the Black Baptist Church, 1880–1920*. Ph.D. diss., University of Rochester, 1984.

Brown Douglas, Kelly. "God Is as Christ Does: Toward a Womanist Theology." *Journal of Religious Thought* 46, no. 1 (1989): 7–16.

——. "To Reflect the Image of God: A Womanist Perspective on Right Relationship and Teaching Womanist Theology." In *Living the Intersection: Womanism and Afrocentrism in Theology*, edited by Cheryl Sanders, 67–77. Minneapolis: Fortress Press, 1995.

Bureau of Labor Statistics, U.S. Department of Labor. *Employment and Unemployment: A Report on 1980*. Special Labor Force Report, 1981, p. 244.

Burroughs, Nannie Helen. *Who Started Women's Day?* Washington, D.C.: Nannie Helen Burroughs, 1968.

Cannon, Katie Geneva. "The Emergence of Black Feminist Consciousness." In *Feminist Interpretation of the Bible*. Edited by Letty Russell. Philadelphia: Westminster Press, 1985.

———. "Surviving the Blight." In *Interpreting Our Mothers' Gardens: Feminist Theology in a Third World Perspective,* edited by Katie Cannon, Ada Maria Isasi-Diaz, Kwok Pui-lan, and Letty Russell, 137–46. Louisville, Ky.: Westminster/John Knox Press, 1988.

Carpenter, Delores Causion. Notes from the National Conference for Ethnic Minority Women in Ministry. Sponsored by the National Council of Churches, Washington, D.C., April 1968.

———. *The Effects of Sect-typeness upon the Professionalization of Black Female M.Div. Graduates, 1972–1984.* Ed.D. diss., Rutgers University, New Brunswick, N.J., 1986.

———. "The Professionalization of the Ministry by Women." *Journal of Religious Thought* 43, no. 1 (1986): 59–75.

———. "Black Women in Religious Institutions: A Historical Summary from Slavery to the 1960s." *Journal of Religious Thought* 46, no. 2 (1990): 7–27.

———. "Women Ministers: Heirs of the Promise–On Fire Under Fire." In *Women: To Preach or Not to Preach,* edited by Ella Pearson Mitchell, 111–17. Valley Forge, Pa.: Judson Press, 1991.

Carroll, Jackson W. "Seminaries and Seminarians: A Study of the Professional Socialization of Protestant Clergymen." Ph.D. diss., Princeton Theological Seminary, 1971.

———. "The Professional Model of Ministry–Is It Worth Saving?" *Theological Education* 21, no. 2 (Spring 1985): 7–48.

———. *As One with Authority: Reflective Leadership in Ministry.* Louisville, Ky.: Westminster/John Knox Press, 1991.

Carroll, Jackson W., Barbara Hargrove, and Adair T. Lummis. *Women of the Cloth: A New Opportunity for Churches.* San Francisco: Harper & Row, 1983.

Carson, Josephine. *Silent Voices: The Southern Negro Woman Today.* New York: Delacorte Press, 1969.

Carter, Norvella, and Matthew Parker, eds. *Women to Women: Perspectives of Fifteen African American Christian Women.* Grand Rapids, Mich.: Zondervan, 1996.

Carter, Ruth C., Willa Curry, Mai H. Gray, Thelma McCallum, and Emma Wilson Strother. *To a Higher Glory: The Growth and Development of Black Women Organized for Mission in the Methodist Church, 1940–1968.* Report of the United Methodist Church (U.S.), Board of Global Ministries, Women's Division, Task Force on the History of the Central Jurisdiction Women's Organization. Cincinnati: The Methodist Church, Education and Cultivation Division, 1968.

Charlton, Joy. "Women Entering the Ordained Ministry: Contradictions and Dilemmas of Status." Paper presented at the meeting of the Society of Scientific Study of Religion, Hartford, Conn., 1978.

Cone, James H., and Gayraud S. Wilmore. *Black Theology: A Documentary History, 1966–1979.* New York: Orbis Books, 1979.

Conrad, Earl. *Harriet Tubman.* Washington, D.C.: Associated Publishers, 1944.

Cornwall Collective. *Your Daughters Shall Prophesy.* New York: Pilgrim Press, 1980.

Daly, Mary. *The Church and the Second Sex.* New York: Harper Colophon, 1975.

Daniels, William Andrew. *The Education of Negro Ministers.* New York: George Doran, 1925.

Day, Helen Cardwell. *Color Ebony.* New York: Sheed and Ward, 1951.

Dodson, Jualynne. "A.M.E. Preaching Women in the Nineteenth Century: Cutting Edge of Women's Inclusion in Church Polity." In *Women in New Worlds: Historical Perspectives on the Wesleyan Tradition,* edited by Hildah Thomas and Rosemary Thomas, 276–89. Nashville: Abingdon Press, 1988.

Epstein, Cynthia. "Positive Effects of the Multiple Negative: Explaining the Success of Black Professional Women." *American Journal of Sociology* 78, no. 4 (January 1973): 917.

Etzioni, Amitai. *The Active Society: A Theory of Societal and Political Processes.* New York: Free Press, 1969.

Fauset, Arthur Huff. *Sojourner Truth: God's Faithful Pilgrim.* Chapel Hill, N.C.: University of North Carolina Press, 1938.

Felder, Cain Hope. *Troubling Biblical Waters: Race, Class and Family.* Maryknoll, N.Y.: Orbis Books, 1989.

Feldman, S. D. "Impediment or Stimulation? Marital Status and Graduate Education." *American Journal of Sociology* 78 (1973): 982–84.

Fiorenza, Elisabeth Schüssler. *Sharing Her Word: Feminist Biblical Interpretation in Context.* Boston: Beacon Press, 1998.

Fischer, Clare Benedicks, Betsy Brenneman, and Anne McGrew Bennett. *Women in a Strange Land.* Philadelphia: Fortress Press, 1975.

Fletcher, John. *Religious Authenticity in the Clergy.* Washington, D.C.: Alban Institute, 1975.

Fukuyama, Yashio. *The Ministry in Transition.* University Park, Penn.: Pennsylvania State University Press, 1972.

Gilbert, Olive. *Narrative of Sojourner Truth: A Bondswoman of Olden Time, with a History of her Labors and Correspondence.* Boston: n.p., 1875.

Gilkes, Cheryl Townsend. "The Role of Women in the Sanctified Church." *Journal of Religious Thought* 43, no. 1 (1986): 24–41.

———. "Together and in Harness." *Signs: Journal of Women in Culture and Society* 10, no. 2 (Summer 1995): 678–99.

———. *If It Wasn't for the Women.* Maryknoll, N.Y.: Orbis Books, 2000.

Gilligan, Carol. *In a Different Voice: Psychological Theory and Women's Development.* Cambridge: Harvard University Press, 1982.

Goode, Gloria Davis. *Preachers of the Word and Singers of the Gospel: The Ministry of Women among Nineteenth Century African Americans.* Ph.D. diss., University of Pennsylvania, 1990.

Grant, Jacquelyn. "Womanist Theology: Black Women's Experience as a Source for Doing Theology, with Special Reference to Christology." *Journal of the Interdenominational Theological Center* 13, no. 2 (1986): 200.

Gray, John. *Men Are from Mars, Women Are from Venus: A Practical Guide for Improving Communication and Getting What You Want in Your Relationships.* San Francisco: HarperCollins, 1992.

Griffin, Arthur D. *By Your Traditions but Not by God's Word: Theological Perspective against Arguments and Actions Opposing and Hindering Women in the Gospel Ministry.* Chicago: Black Light Fellowship, 1993.

Grimke, Charlotte Forten. "Letter to the Editor." In *The Life and Writings of the Grimke Family.* Edited by Anna J. Cooper. Vol. 2 (1951): 97.

Gustafson, James. "Professions as Callings." *The Social Service Review* 56 (1982): 514.

Hall, Judith A. *Nonverbal Sex Difference: Accuracy of Communication and Expressive Style.* Baltimore: Johns Hopkins University Press, 1984.

Hamilton, Charles V. *The Black Preacher in America.* New York: William Morrow, 1972.

Hammond, J. M. "Biography Building to Insure the Future: Women's Negotiation of Gender Relevancy in Medical School." *Symbolic Interaction* 3 (1980): 35–49.

Hardesty, Nancy. "Women and the Seminaries–Women Clergy: How Their Presence Is Changing the Church." *Christian Century* (February 1979): 122–23.

Harrison, Beverly Wildung. "Sexism and the Contemporary Church: When Evasion Becomes Complicity." In *Sexist Religion and Women in the Church: No More Silence!* ed. Alice L. Hageman, 195–216. New York: Association Press, 1974.

Hedgeman, Anna Arnold. *The Trumpet Sounds.* New York: Holt, Rinehart, and Winston, 1964.

Height, Dorothy I., and J. Oscar Lee. *The Christian Citizen and Civil Rights: A Guide to Study and Action.* New York: The Women's Press, National Board of the YWCA, and the Department of Race Relations of the Federal Church of Christ in America, 1948.

Helsinger, Elizabeth K., Robin Lauterbach Sheets, and William Veeder. "The Woman Question: Society and Literature in Britain and America 1837–1883." In *Social Issues* 2. Chicago: University of Chicago Press, 1983.

Hewitt, Emily C., and Suzanne Hiatt. *Women Priests: Yes or No.* New York: Seabury Press, 1973.

Hiatt, Suzanne. "Women clergy: how their presence is changing the church: A symposium on the seminary campus." *Christian Century* (February 1979): 124–25.

Higginbotham, Evelyn Brooks. *Righteous Discontent: The Women's Movement in the Black Baptist Church, 1880–1920.* Cambridge, Mass.: Harvard University Press, 1993.

hooks, bell. *Sisters of the Yam: Black Women and Self-Recovery.* Boston: South End Press, 1993.

Horner, Martina S. "Fail: Bright Women," *Psychology Today* (3 Nov. 1969): 36–38.

Hughes, Everett Cheerington. "Professions." In *The Sociological Eye: Selected Papers*, edited by E. C. Hughes. Chicago: Aldine, 1971; New Brunswick, N.J.: Transaction Books, 1984.

Imbler, John M., and Linda K. Plengemeier. *Discerning the Call: Advancing the Quality of Ordained Leadership.* St. Louis: Chalice Press, 1992.

Jacquet, Constant H., Jr. *Women Ministers in 1977.* New York: Office of Research, Evaluation, and Planning of the National Council of Churches (March 1978).

James, Janet Wilson, ed. *Women in American Religion.* Philadelphia: University of Pennsylvania Press, 1980.

Jeness, Mary. *Twelve Negro Americans.* New York: Friendship Press, 1936.

Johnson, Suzan D., ed. *Wise Women Bearing Gifts: Joys and Struggles of Their Faith.* Valley Forge, Penn.: Judson Press, 1988.

Jones, Arthur R., and Lee Taylor. "Differential Recruitment of Female Professionals: A Case Study of Clergywomen." Paper presented at the annual meeting of the Southern Sociological Society, Atlanta, Ga. (April 1965).

Kanter, Rosabeth Moss. "Some Effects of Proportions on Group Life: Skewed Sex Ratios and Responses to Token Women." *American Journal of Sociology* 82 (1977): 965–90.

Kanter, Rosabeth Moss, and M. Millman. *Another Voice.* Garden City, N.Y.: Doubleday, 1975.

Kleinman, Sherryl. "Women in Seminary: Dilemmas of Professional Socialization." *Sociology of Education* 57 (October 1984): 210–19.

Kroeger, Richard Clark, and Catherine Clark Kroeger. *I Suffer Not a Woman: Rethinking 1 Timothy 2:11–15 in Light of Ancient Evidence.* Grand Rapids, Mich.: Baker Book House, 1992.

Kunjufu, Jwanza. *The Power, Passion, and Pain of Black Love.* Chicago: African American Images, 1993.

Lee, Jarena. *Religious Experience and Journal of Mrs. Jarena Lee: Giving an Account of her Call to Preach the Gospel.* Philadelphia: n.p., 1849.

Lehman, Edward C. *Project S.W.I.M.: A Study of Women in Ministry. A Research Repost to the Ministers Council.* Valley Forge, Penn.: American Baptist Churches, 1979.

——. "Organizational Resistance to Women in Ministry." *Sociological Review* 24 (1981): 236–55.

Lerner, Gerda. *Black Women in White America.* New York: Vintage, 1972.

Lincoln, C. Eric, and Lawrence H. Mamiya. *The Black Church in the African American Experience.* Durham, N.C.: Duke University Press, 1990.

Lyles, Jean Coffey. "United Methodist Women Clergy: Sisterhood and Survival." *Christian Century* (February 1979): 117–19.

McAfee, Sara J. "History of the Women's Missionary Society." *Christian Phoenix Herald.* New York: Schomberg Library, C.M.E. Church, 1945.

McKenzie, Vashti. *Not Without a Struggle: Leadership Development for African American Women in Ministry.* Cleveland: United Church Press, 1996.

Meyers, William. *The Irresistible Urge To Preach: A Collection of African American "Call" Stories.* Atlanta: Aaron Press, 1992.

Mitchell, Ella Pearson, ed. *Those Preaching Women.* Vols. 1 and 2. Valley Forge, Penn.: Judson Press, 1988.

Mitchell, Juliet. *Woman's Estate.* New York: Vintage Books, 1971.

Moore, Wilbert E. *The Professions: Roles and Rules.* New York: Russell Sage, 1970.

Murray, Pauli. *States' Laws on Race and Color.* New York: Women's Division of Christian Service, Board of Missions of the Methodist Church, 1951.

———. *Song in a Weary Throat.* New York: Harper & Row, 1987.

Muto, Susan. *Womanspirit: Reclaiming the Deep Feminine in Our Human Spirituality.* New York: Crossroad, 1991.

Newman, Barbara. *Sister Wisdom: St. Hildegard's Theology of the Feminine.* Berkeley, Calif.: University of California Press, 1987.

Newsome, Clarence C. "Mary McLeod Bethune as Religionist." In *Women in New Worlds: Historical Perspectives on the Wesleyan Tradition,* vol. 1, edited by Rosemary S. Keller and Hildah F. Thomas, 102–16. Nashville: Abingdon Press, 1981.

———. "Mary McLeod Bethune in Religious Perspective: A Seminal Essay." Ph.D. diss., Duke University, 1982.

Noren, Carol M. *The Woman in the Pulpit.* Nashville: Abingdon Press, 1991.

Ogburn, William F. *Social Change.* New York: B. W. Huebsch, 1922.

Ortiz, Victoria. *Sojourner Truth: A Self-Made Woman.* Philadelphia: J. P. Lippincott, 1974.

Osborn, Ronald E. *The Education of Ministers for the Coming Age.* St. Louis: Christian Board of Publication, 1987.

Pauli, Hertha. *Her Name Was Truth.* New York: Appleton-Century-Crofts, 1962.

Pleck, J. H. "The Work Family Role System." In *Women and Work,* edited by R. Kahn-Hut, A. K. Daniels, and R. Colvard, 101–10. New York: Oxford University Press, 1982.

Podmore, D., and A. Spencer. "Women Lawyers in England: The Experience of Inequality." *Work and Occupations* 9 (1982): 337–61.

Pope, Liston. *Millhands and Preachers: A Study of Gastonia.* New Haven, Conn.: Yale University Press, 1942.

Powell, Adam Clayton, Jr. *Marching Blacks.* Charlotte, N.C.: A.M.E. Zion, 1974.

Regional Christian Women's Fellowship. *Women in Ministry in Virginia.* Christian Church (Disciples of Christ) in Virginia, 1996.

Roberts, J. Deotis. "The Black Caucus and the Failure of Christian Theology." *Journal of Religious Thought* 26, no. 2 (Summer 1969): 15–25.

———. "The Hermeneutic Circle of Black Theology." In *Black Theology Today: Liberation and Contextualization,* 3–33. New York: Edwin Mellen Press, 1983.

Rooks, Shelby. *Revolution in Zion: History of the Fund for Theological Education*. Philadelphia: Pilgrim Press, 1982.

Ruether, Rosemary Radford, and Eleanor McLaughlin. *Women of Spirit*. New York: Simon and Schuster, 1979.

Russell, Letty M., Kwok Pui-lan, Ada Maria Isasi-Diaz, and Katie G. Canon. *Inheriting Our Mothers' Gardens: Feminist Theology in Third World Perspective*. Louisville: Westminister Press, 1988.

Sanders, Cheryl J. "The Woman as Preacher." *Journal of Religious Thought* 43, no. 1 (1986): 6–23.

——. "Womanist Ethics: Contemporary Trends and Themes." Paper presented at the Annual Meeting of the Society of Christian Ethics, 1994.

——. *Living the Intersection: Womanism and Afrocentrism in Theology*. Minneapolis: Fortress Press, 1995.

——. *Ministry at the Margins: The Prophetic Mission of Women, Youth & the Poor*. Downers Grove, Ill.: Intervarsity Press, 1997.

Schuller, D. S., M. L. Brekke, and M. P. Strommen. *Readiness for Ministry,* vol. 1. Vandalia, Ohio: Association of Theological Schools in the U.S. and Canada, 1975.

Sellers, Karen Smith. "When the Pastor Is a Woman." *A. D. Magazine* (1979): 15–18.

Sennett, R. *The Fall of Public Man: On the Social Psychology of Capitalism*. New York: Vintage, 1978.

Smith, Amanda. *The Story of the Lord's Dealing with Mrs. Amanda Smith, Colored Evangelist*. Reprinted with new introduction by Jualynne Dodson. New York: Oxford University Press, 1988.

Stagg, Evelyn, and Frank Stagg. *Women in the World of Jesus*. Philadelphia: Westminster Press, 1978.

Stewart, Maria. *Productions of Mrs. Maria Stewart*. Boston: Friends of Freedom and Virtue, 1835.

Tate, Deborah. "It's Terrific." WYCB-AM radio program, Washington, D.C. (May 1983).

Taylor, Marvin, ed. *Fact Book on Theological Education: An Annual Report of the Association of Theological Schools in the United States and Canada*. Vandalia, Ohio: Association of Theological Schools, 1984.

Townes, Emilie M. *A Troublin' in My Soul: Womanist Perspectives on Evil and Suffering*. Maryknoll, N.Y.: Orbis Press, 1993.

Truth, Sojourner. *Narrative of Sojourner, A Northern Slave*. Boston: n.p., 1850.

Vale, G. *Fanaticism: Its Influence, Illustrated by The Simple Narrative of Isabella in the Case of Matthias, Mr. & Mrs. B. Folger, Mr. Mills, Catherine Isabella etc*. New York: G. Vale, 1835.

Van Kaam, Adrianne. *On Being Yourself: Reflections on Spirituality and Originality.* Denville, N.J.: Dimension Books, 1972.

Van Scoyoc, Nancy J. *Women, Change, and the Church.* Nashville: Abingdon Press, 1980.

Walker, Alice. *In Search of Our Mothers' Gardens: Womanist Prose.* New York: Harcourt Brace, 1983.

Wallston, B. S., M. A. Foster, and M. Berger. "I Will Follow Him—Myth, Reality, or Forced Choice: Job Seeking Experiences of Dual Career Couples." *Psychology of Women Quarterly* 3 (1978): 9–21.

Washington, Joseph. *Black Sects and Cults.* Garden City, N.Y.: Doubleday/Anchor Books, 1973.

Weber, Max. *Economy and Society.* New York: Bedminster Press, 1968.

Weems, Renita. *Just a Sister Away: A Womanist Vision of Women's Relationships in the Bible.* San Diego: LuraMedia, 1988.

Williams, Delores S. "The Color of Feminism: Or Speaking the Black Woman's Tongue." *The Journal of Religious Thought* 42, no. 1 (1986): 42–58.

——. "Womanist Theology: Black Women's Voices." *Christianity and Crisis* 47, no. 3 (March 2, 1987): 66–70.

——. *Sisters in the Wilderness: The Challenge of Womanist God-Talk.* Maryknoll, N.Y.: Orbis Books, 1993.

Winter, Miriam Therese. *WomanWord: A Feminist Lectionary and Psalter for Women.* New York: Crossroad Publishing, 1994.

Winter, Miriam Therese, Adair Lummis, and Allison Stokes. *Defecting in Place: Women Claiming Responsibility for Their Own Spiritual Lives.* New York: Crossroad Publishing, 1994.

Wortman, John. "Seeing Light on the Edge of the Wilderness: The Professional Development of African American Women Divinity Graduates." Unpublished senior thesis, Carlton College, Minnesota, 1996.

Young, Viola Mae. *Little Helps for Pastors and Members.* Rosebud, Ala.: n.p., 1909.

Zikmund, Barbara Brown, Adair T. Lummis, Patricia Mei Yin Chang. *Clergywomen: An Uphill Calling.* Louisville, Ky.: Westminster John Knox Press, 1998.

Subject Index

Abraham 78
Africa 3–4, 6, 8, 33, 48, 78, 87, 103, 106, 145
African Methodist Episcopal 1, 3, 7, 11, 18, 35–36, 65, 103, 117, 135, 137–39, 142–44, 169, 174
African Methodist Episcopal Zion 18, 65, 138–39, 142–44, 69
Alban Institute 92
Allen, Richard 3–4, 35
A.M.E. (*See* African Methodist Episcopal)
American Academy of Religion 104
American Baptists 52, 55, 65, 86, 135–38, 142–44, 169
American Indian 16
American Protestantism 67
A.M.E.Z. (*See* African Methodist Episcopal Zion)
Amos, Barbara 178
Andrews, William L. 1
Association of Theological Schools xi–xii, 11–12, 86, 133
ATS (*See* Association a Theological Schools)
authority
  biblical 66
  charismatic 33, 67
  professional 33
  rational-legal 67
  sacred and secular 61
  traditional 67

Baptist 6, 34, 36, 78, 101, 113, 138, 154
  American 52, 55, 135–39, 142–44, 169
  Missionary 135, 137–39, 142–44, 152
  National 13, 18, 25–26, 89, 96, 135–39, 142–44
  Progressive 138–39, 142–43
  Southern 138, 142–44, 180
  women 7–8
Barber, Bernard 30
Becker, Howard 29
Benjamin Mays Fellowship xi
Bethlehem Center 10
Bethune, Mary McLeod 11, 93, 103
Bible/biblical 3, 16, 19, 21, 23, 29– 30, 38, 53, 62, 84–85, 104, 170, 179
bishop
  Amos, Barbara 178
  Fisher, Violet 14
  Harris, Barbara 14
  Kelley, Leontyne 14
  Lee, Linda 14

McKenzie, Vashti 14
Robinson, Ida B. 169
Shamana, Beverly 14
women 14
black women in the ministry
  contemporary images 21–23
  nineteenth century 2–6
  twentieth century 6–10
Brown-Douglas, Kelly 105
Bryan, Andrew 35
Burroughs, Nannie Helen 2, 8–9, 93

Cannon, Katie 104
career goals 72–74
Carroll, Jackson 31
Carter, Jimmy 180
Christian education 10–14
Christian Methodist Episcopal 11, 18, 65, 138–39, 142–43, 169
Church of God in Christ 18, 21, 35, 137–39, 142–44
churches 151
clergy couples 57–58
C.M.E. (*See* Christian Methodist Episcopal)
C.O.G.I.C. (*See* Church of God in Christ)
Commission on Religion 90
Commission on the Status of Women 90
Congress of National Black Churches 97, 169
cultural lag 65–66

Daniels, A. W. 35
Day, Helen Caldwell 13
deaconess 7, 14, 19, 23
Delk, Yvonne 14
denominations 100–103, 137–40
Diaconal Ministry 90
Dodson, Jualynne 1
Drew University 23
Duke University Divinity School 65, 134

Elaw, Zepha 1, 96
employment 68–72
Esther 78
Eugene, Toinette xvi

Fact Book on Theological Education 63–64
Farrakhan, Louis 180
Fisher, Violet 14
Fletcher, John 33
Foote, Julia 1, 96
Forbes, James 162
Franklin, C. L. 162

Freedmen's
  Aid Society 6
  Board 6
  Bureau 4
FTC (*See* Fund for Theological Education)
Fukuyama, Yashio 29–31
Fund for Theological Education xi

Gandhi, Mahatma 118
Garrett Evangelical Theological Seminary 65
Gilkes, Cheryl Townsend xv, 1
God 3, 13, 31, 62, 81, 92, 97, 104, 111–12,
    126, 163, 165, 167, 176–80
  anointing of 126, 163, 167
  attributes of 62, 110–11, 113–15, 166
  belief in 91
  call of 41, 97, 112, 126
  compassion of 61
  as creator 48, 76, 110
  existential knowledge of 33
  faith in 86
  as father 15
  as friend 110, 114–15
  as healer 110, 114–15
  as helper 110
  images of 15, 60, 62, 81, 91, 105, 110,
    113–15, 120, 129, 164–68
  kingdom of 78, 179
  as liberator 110
  male referent for 76
  minister's relationship to 33
  as mother 164
  as presence 110, 113, 115
  presence of 15, 61
  purpose of 111, 126
  as Spirit 110, 111, 114–15
  voice of 105
  as wisdom 110, 111, 114–15
Goode, Gloria Davis 96
Grant, Jacquelyn 23, 104
graying of the clergy xiii
Grimke, Charlotte Forten 4

Hagar 78
Hall, Anna 7
Hamilton, Charles V. xii, 35, 37
Hargis, Hattie 10
Hedgeman, Anna Arnold 13
Height, Dorothy 12
Hicks, H. Beecher 162
Holy Spirit 20, 60, 62, 86, 97, 111–14, 116,
    166–68
Hood College 134
Hoover, Theresa 14

Howard University School of Divinity xi, xv–
    xvi, 20–21, 23, 64–65, 93, 104–6, 134, 145
Hoyt, Thomas xv

India 5, 78
Interdenominational Theological Center
    xi, 23, 65, 104, 106, 134, 145
Ishmael 78

Jakes, T. D. 141, 162
Jeness, Mary 10–12
job market 55–57
Jones, Lawrence xvi, 64, 104
Joseph 78
Journal of Feminist Studies in Religion 105

Kelley, Leontyne 14, 23
Kenya 87, 106, 145
King, Jr., Martin Luther 126, 162, 171

leadership positions 87
Lee, Jarena 1, 3–4, 96, 112
Lee, Linda 14
liberation theology 48, 86
Lille, George 35
Lilly Endowment xi, 47
Lummis, Adair xv, 38, 64, 94, 169
Lutheran 34, 39, 52, 138–39, 142–44

McKenzie, Vashti 14
marital status 107–8, 141–45
Mason, Denise xv
mentors (*See* role models)
Methodists (*See also* United Methodist,
    A.M.E., A.M.E.Z., C.M.E.) 21, 34, 65,
    86, 137, 169
Meyers, William 145
Middle East 78
minister
  education 35–37
  licensing 35
ministry
  call to xii
  education 35–37
  gender differences 163
  multiple tasks 160–61
  practice of 110
  as a profession 29–32
  professional model of 31–35
  social issues 165
  women in 49–54
Moore, Wilbert E. 33
Moseley, Matilda 10
Murphy, Sarah D. 11
Murray, Pauli 2, 12, 17